Veloce *Classic Reprint* **Series**

MOTOR RACING

Reflections of a lost era

Dedication

To all those who gave we enthusiasts so much to remember.

Also from Veloce Publishing:

Speedpro Series
4-Cylinder Engine Short Block High-Performance Manual – New Updated & Revised Edition (Hammill)
Alfa Romeo DOHC High-performance Manual (Kartalamakis)
Alfa Romeo V6 Engine High-performance Manual (Kartalamakis)
BMC 998cc A-series Engine, How to Power Tune (Hammill)
1275cc A-series High-performance Manual (Hammill)
Camshafts – How to Choose & Time Them For Maximum Power (Hammill)
Competition Car Datalogging Manual, The (Templeman)
Cylinder Heads, How to Build, Modify & Power Tune – Updated & Revised Edition (Burgess & Gollan)
Distributor-type Ignition Systems, How to Build & Power Tune – New 3rd Edition (Hammill)
Fast Road Car, How to Plan and Build – Revised & Updated Colour New Edition (Stapleton)
Ford SOHC 'Pinto' & Sierra Cosworth DOHC Engines, How to Power Tune – Updated & Enlarged Edition (Hammill)
Ford V8, How to Power Tune Small Block Engines (Hammill)
Harley-Davidson Evolution Engines, How to Build & Power Tune (Hammill)
Holley Carburetors, How to Build & Power Tune – Revised & Updated Edition (Hammill)
Honda Civic Type R High-Performance Manual, The (Cowland & Clifford)
Jaguar XK Engines, How to Power Tune – Revised & Updated Colour Edition (Hammill)
Land Rover Discovery, Defender & Range Rover – How to Modify Coil Sprung Models for High Performance & Off-Road Action (Hosier)
MG Midget & Austin-Healey Sprite, How to Power Tune – Enlarged & updated 4th Edition (Stapleton)
MGB 4-cylinder Engine, How to Power Tune (Burgess)
MGB V8 Power, How to Give Your – Third Colour Edition (Williams)
MGB, MGC & MGB V8, How to Improve – New 2nd Edition (Williams)
Mini Engines, How to Power Tune On a Small Budget – Colour Edition (Hammill)
Motorcycle-engined Racing Car, How to Build (Pashley)
Motorsport, Getting Started in (Collins)
Nissan GT-R High-performance Manual, The (Gorodji)
Nitrous Oxide High-performance Manual, The (Langfield)
Race & Trackday Driving Techniques (Hornsey)
Retro or classic car for high performance, How to modify your (Stapleton)
Rover V8 Engines, How to Power Tune (Hammill)
Secrets of Speed – Today's techniques for 4-stroke engine blueprinting & tuning (Swager)
Sportscar & Kitcar Suspension & Brakes, How to Build & Modify – Revised 3rd Edition (Hammill)
SU Carburettor High-performance Manual (Hammill)
Successful Low-Cost Rally Car, How to Build a (Young)
Suzuki 4x4, How to Modify For Serious Off-road Action (Richardson)
Tiger Avon Sportscar, How to Build Your Own – Updated & Revised 2nd Edition (Dudley)
TR2, 3 & TR4, How to Improve (Williams)
TR5, 250 & TR6, How to Improve (Williams)
TR7 & TR8, How to Improve (Williams)
V8 Engine, How to Build a Short Block For High Performance (Hammill)
Volkswagen Beetle Suspension, Brakes & Chassis, How to Modify For High Performance (Hale)
Volkswagen Bus Suspension, Brakes & Chassis for High Performance, How to Modify – Updated & Enlarged New Edition (Hale)
Weber DCOE, & Dellorto DHLA Carburetors, How to Build & Power Tune – 3rd Edition (Hammill)

Those Were The Days ... Series
Alpine Trials & Rallies 1910-1973 (Pfundner)
American 'Independent' Automakers – AMC to Willys 1945 to 1960 (Mort)
Anglo-American Cars from the 1930s to the 1970s (Mort)
Austerity Motoring (Bobbitt)
Austins, The last real (Peck)
Brighton National Speed Trials (Gardiner)
British and European Trucks of the 1970s (Peck)
British Drag Racing – The early years (Pettitt)
British Touring Car Racing (Collins)
Drag Bike Racing in Britain – From the mid '60s to the mid '80s (Lee)
Endurance Racing at Silverstone in the 1970s & 1980s (Parker)
Hot Rod & Stock Car Racing in Britain in the 1980s (Neil)
Last Real Austins 1946-1959, The (Peck)
MG's Abingdon Factory (Moylan)
Motor Racing at Brands Hatch in the Seventies (Parker)
Motor Racing at Brands Hatch in the Eighties (Parker)
Motor Racing at Crystal Palace (Collins)
Motor Racing at Goodwood in the Sixties (Gardiner)
Motor Racing at Nassau in the 1950s & 1960s (O'Neil)
Motor Racing at Oulton Park in the 1960s (McFadyen)
Motor Racing at Oulton Park in the 1970s (McFadyen)
Motor Racing at Thruxton in the 1970s (Grant-Braham)
Motor Racing at Thruxton in the 1980s (Grant-Braham)
Superprix – The Story of Birmingham Motor Race (Page & Collins)

Great Cars
Austin-Healey – A celebration of the fabulous 'Big' Healey (Piggott)
Triumph TR - TR2 to 6: The last of the traditional sports cars (Piggott)

Rally Giants Series
Audi Quattro (Robson)
Austin Healey 100-6 & 3000 (Robson)
Fiat 131 Abarth (Robson)
Ford Escort MkI (Robson)
Ford Escort RS Cosworth & World Rally Car (Robson)
Ford Escort RS1800 (Robson)
Lancia Delta 4WD/Integrale (Robson)
Lancia Stratos (Robson)
Mini Cooper/Mini Cooper S (Robson)
Peugeot 205 T16 (Robson)
Saab 96 & V4 (Robson)
Subaru Impreza (Robson)
Toyota Celica GT4 (Robson)

WSC Giants
Audi R8 (Wagstaff)
Ferrari 312P & 312PB (Collins & McDonough)
Gulf-Mirage 1967 to 1982 (McDonough)
Matra Sports Cars – MS620, 630, 650, 660 & 670 – 1966 to 1974 (McDonough)

Biographies
A Chequered Life – Graham Warner and the Chequered Flag (Hesletine)
A Life Awheel – The 'auto' biography of W de Forte (Skelton)
Amédée Gordini ... a true racing legend (Smith)
André Lefebvre, and the cars he created at Voisin and Citroën (Beck)
Chris Carter at Large – Stories from a lifetime in motorcycle racing (Carter & Skelton)
Cliff Allison, The Official Biography of – From the Fells to Ferrari (Gauld)
Edward Turner – The Man Behind the Motorcycles (Clew)
Driven by Desire – The Desiré Wilson Story
First Principles – The Official Biography of Keith Duckworth (Burr)
Inspired to Design – F1 cars, Indycars & racing tyres: the autobiography of Nigel Bennett (Bennett)
Jack Sears, The Official Biography of – Gentleman Jack (Gauld)
Jim Redman – 6 Times World Motorcycle Champion: The Autobiography (Redman)
John Chatham – 'Mr Big Healey' – The Official Biography (Burr)
The Lee Noble Story (Wilkins)
Mason's Motoring Mayhem – Tony Mason's hectic life in motorsport and television (Mason)
Raymond Mays' Magnificent Obsession (Apps)
Pat Moss Carlsson Story, The – Harnessing Horsepower (Turner)
'Sox' – Gary Hocking – the forgotten World Motorcycle Champion (Hughes)
Tony Robinson – The biography of a race mechanic (Wagstaff)
Virgil Exner – Visioneer: The Official Biography of Virgil M Exner Designer Extraordinaire (Grist)

General
11/2-litre GP Racing 1961-1965 (Whitelock)
AC Two-litre Saloons & Buckland Sportscars (Archibald)
Alfa Romeo 155/156/147 Competition Touring Cars (Collins)
Alfa Romeo Montreal – The dream car that came true (Taylor)
Alfa Tipo 33 (McDonough & Collins)
Alpine & Renault – The Development of the Revolutionary Turbo F1 Car 1968 to 1979 (Smith)
Anatomy of the Works Minis (Moylan)
Autodrome (Collins & Ireland)
Automotive A-Z, Lane's Dictionary of Automotive Terms (Lane)
Bahamas Speed Weeks, The (O'Neil)
BMC Competitions Department Secrets (Turner, Chambers & Browning)
BMW 5-Series (Cranswick)
BMW Z-Cars (Taylor)
British at Indianapolis, The (Wagstaff)
British Cars, The Complete Catalogue of, 1895-1975 (Culshaw & Horrobin)
BRM – A Mechanic's Tale (Salmon)
Bugatti Type 57 Grand Prix – A Celebration (Tomlinson)
Carrera Panamericana, La (Tipler)
Car-tastrophes – 80 automotive atrocities from the past 20 years (Honest John, Fowler)
Competition Car Aerodynamics 3rd Edition (McBeath)
Cortina – Ford's Bestseller (Robson)
Cosworth - The Search for Power (6th edition) (Robson)
Coventry Climax Racing Engines (Hammill)
Daily Mirror 1970 World Cup Rally 40, The (Robson)
Daimler SP250 New Edition (Long)
Datsun Fairlady Roadster to 280ZX – The Z-Car Story (Long)
Dino – The V6 Ferrari (Long)
Dodge Challenger & Plymouth Barracuda (Grist)
Dodge Charger – Enduring Thunder (Ackerson)
Dodge Dynamite! (Grist)
Drive on the Wild Side, A – 20 Extreme Driving Adventures From Around the World (Weaver)
East German Motor Vehicles in Pictures (Suhr/Weinreich)
Fast Ladies – Female Racing Drivers 1888 to 1970 (Bouzanquet)
Ferrari 288 GTO, The Book of the (Sackey)
Ferrari 333 SP (O'Neil)
Fiat & Abarth 124 Spider & Coupé (Tipler)
Fiats, Great Small (Ward)
Ford GT – Then, and Now (Streather)
Ford GT40 (Legate)
Ford Midsize Muscle – Fairlane, Torino & Ranchero (Cranswick)
Ford Model Y (Roberts)
Formula 5000 Motor Racing, Back then ... and back now (Lawson)
Forza Minardi! (Vigar)
Grand Prix Ferrari – The Years of Enzo Ferrari's Power, 1948-1980 (Pritchard)
Grand Prix Ford – DFV-powered Formula 1 Cars (Robson)
GT – The World's Best GT Cars 1953-73 (Dawson)
Hillclimbing & Sprinting – The Essential Manual (Short & Wilkinson)
Honda NSX (Long)
Jaguar, The Rise of (Price)
Jaguar XJ 220 – The Inside Story (Moreton)
Jaguar XJ-S, The Book of the (Long)
Kris Meeke – Intercontinental Rally Challenge Champion (McBride)
Lamborghini Miura Bible, The (Sackey)
Lancia 037 (Collins)
Lancia Delta HF Integrale (Blaettel & Wagner)
Le Mans Panoramic (Ireland)
Lexus Story, The (Long)
Lola – The Illustrated History (1957-1977) (Starkey)
Lola – All the Sports Racing & Single-seater Racing Cars 1978-1997 (Starkey)
Lotus 18 Colin Chapman's U-turn (Whitelock)
Lotus 49 (Oliver)
Maserati 250F In Focus (Pritchard)
Mazda MX-5 Miata Roadster (Long)
Maximum Mini (Booij)
Mercedes-Benz W123-series – All models 1976 to 1986 (Long)
Mitsubishi Lancer Evo, The Road Car & WRC Story (Long)
Montlhéry, The Story of the Paris Autodrome (Boddy)
Motor Racing – The Pursuit of Victory 1930-1962 (Carter)
Motor Racing – The Pursuit of Victory 1963-1972 (Wyatt/Sears)
Motor Racing Heroes – The Stories of 100 Greats (Newman)
Motorcycle GP Racing in the 1960s (Pereira)
Motorsport In colour, 1950s (Wainwright)
MV Agusta Fours, The book of the classic (Falloon)
N.A.R.T. – A concise history of the North American Racing Team 1957 to 1983 (O'Neil)
Nissan 300ZX & 350Z – The Z-Car Story (Long)
Nissan GT-R Supercar: Born to race (Gorodji)
Northeast American Sports Car Races 1950-1959 (O'Neil)
Pontiac Firebird – New 3rd Edition (Cranswick)
Porsche Boxster (Long)
Porsche 908 (Födisch, Neßhöver, Roßbach, Schwarz & Roßbach)
Porsche 911 Carrera – The Last of the Evolution (Corlett)
Porsche 911R, RS & RSR, 4th Edition (Starkey)
Porsche 911, The Book of the (Long)
The Porsche 924 Carreras – evolution to excellence (Smith)
Porsche 996 'Supreme Porsche' – The Essential Companion (Streather)
Porsche 997 2004-2012 – Porsche Excellence (Streather)
Porsche Racing Cars – 1953 to 1975 (Long)
Porsche Racing Cars – 1976 to 2005 (Long)
Porsche – The Rally Story (Meredith)
RAC Rally Action! (Gardiner)
RACING COLOURS – MOTOR RACING COMPOSITIONS 1908-2009 (Newman)
Roads with a View – England's greatest views and how to find them by road (Corfield)
Runways & Racers (O'Neil)
Subaru Impreza: The Road Car And WRC Story (Long)
Supercar, How to Build your own (Thompson)
To Boldly Go – twenty six vehicle designs that dared to be different (Hull)
Toyota Celica & Supra, The Book of Toyota's Sports Coupés (Long)
Toyota MR2 Coupés & Spyders (Long)
Unraced (Collins)
VW – The Air-cooled Era (Copping)
Works Minis, The Last (Purves & Brenchley)
Works Rally Mechanic (Moylan)

www.veloce.co.uk

First published in 2005 by Veloce Publishing Limited, Veloce House, Parkway Farm Business Park, Middle Farm Way, Poundbury, Dorchester DT1 3AR, England.
Fax 01305 250479 / e-mail info@veloce.co.uk / web www.veloce.co.uk or www.velocebooks.com.
Reprinted July 2017 and April 2019. ISBN 978-1-787115-23-1. UPC: 6-36847-01523-7
© Anthony Carter and Veloce Publishing 2005, 2007, 2017 & 2019. All rights reserved. With the exception of quoting brief passages for the purpose of review, no part of this publication may be recorded, reproduced or transmitted by any means, including photocopying, without the written permission of Veloce Publishing Ltd. Throughout this book logos, model names and designations, etc, have been used for the purposes of identification, illustration and decoration. Such names are the property of the trademark holder as this is not an official publication.
Readers with ideas for automotive books, or books on other transport or related hobby subjects, are invited to write to the editorial director of Veloce Publishing at the above address.
British Library Cataloguing in Publication Data - A catalogue record for this book is available from the British Library. Typesetting, design and page make-up all by Veloce Publishing Ltd on Apple Mac.
Printed and bound by CPI Group (UK) Ltd, Croydon, CR0 4YY.

Veloce *Classic Reprint* Series

MOTOR RACING
Reflections of a lost era
Anthony Carter

VELOCE PUBLISHING
THE PUBLISHER OF FINE AUTOMOTIVE BOOKS

Contents

Preface 5
Acknowledgements 5
Bibliography 6
Foreword 7

The Fifties **9**
   Early days 9
   Back to civvy street 11
   Of cars and cameras 13
   Vanwall versus BRM 15
   Safety? – what's that? 19
   Triumph and tragedy 20

5th August 1956, The German GP, Nürburgring 24
3rd May 1958, *Daily Express* International Trophy,
   Silverstone 28
21-22 June 1958, *Vingt Quatre Heures,* Le Mans 31
19th July 1958, British Grand Prix, Silverstone 41
2nd May 1959, *Daily Express* International Trophy,
   Silverstone 41

The Sixties **42**
   A new era 42
   Following the races 44
   Mike Parkes 49
   David and Goliath 50
   Gas turbine interlude 51
   On the road 53
   Chaos at Reims 56
   Dragsters 59
   Big bangers 59
   Unprepared … again! 61
   Maranello 62
   Changing times 63
   'Wing things' 64
   To conclude … 68

14th May 1960, *Daily Express* International Trophy,
   Silverstone 70
6th May 1961, *Daily Express* International Trophy,
   Silverstone 77
14th April 1962, International Lombank Trophy Meeting,
   Snetterton 78
12th May 1962, *Daily Express* International Trophy,
   Silverstone 79
1st July 1962, Grand Prix (non-championship) de Reims . . 85
8th July 1962, French Grand Prix, Rouen-les-Essarts 95
6th August 1962, International Guards Trophy, Brands
   Hatch 100
6th October 1962, *The Motor* International Six Hours
   Saloon Car Race, Brands Hatch 109
11th May 1963, *Daily Express* International Trophy,
   Silverstone 113
15th-16th June 1963, *Vingt Quatre Heures,* Le Mans 121
23rd June 1963, Dutch Grand Prix, Zandvoort 135
7th-8th July 2001, Festival of Speed, Goodwood 137
30th June 1963, French Grand Prix, Reims 137
September 2001, Reims revisited 144
20th July 1963, British Grand Prix, Silverstone 146
5th Aug 1963, International Guards Trophy Meeting,
   Brands Hatch 148
16th July 1966, British Grand Prix, Brands Hatch 151
29th August 1966, International Guards Trophy
   Meeting, Brands Hatch 154
June 1967, Ferrari Factory, Maranello, ... 161
1995, Ferrari Factory, Maranello, ... 165
7th July 1968, French Grand Prix, Rouen-les-Essarts 166
1999, Rouen-les-Essarts, revisited 181

The Sequel **182**
   18th March 1973, Race of Champions, Brands Hatch 183
   14th July 1973, British Grand Prix, Silverstone 184
   20th July 1974, British Grand Prix, Brands Hatch 184
   14th July 1979, British Grand Prix, Silverstone 195
   Miscellaneous memorabilia 197
   10th July 1965, British Grand Prix, Silverstone 200

Index **204**

Preface

This book is a personal story, in words and pictures, of motor racing in the golden age, the 1950s, 1960s and 1970s, told entirely from an enthusiast's point of view.

In those days, motor racing was a noble and sometimes brutal sport, played out on a world stage scarcely recognisable today. It was also a sport which was accessible. At Silverstone, the Nürburgring, Le Mans, and Reims, for example, places I had initially only dreamt about, I was able to simply walk into the paddock, with a little subterfuge on occasion, to take the photographs you see here, and talk to fellow enthusiasts and the important players of the day.

Although this is a collection of personal reflections, I hope the book will rekindle long forgotten memories for the older enthusiast, and demonstrate to the younger generation how much more personal the involvement was before television and sponsorship changed the sport forever.

Acknowledgements

I am forever indebted to my son Damian, without whose inspiration this work would never have been started, and to my wife Vyvian without whose encouragement, ideas and hours spent at the keyboard it would most certainly never have been finished!

I am especially grateful to A. David Owen, OBE, Chairman, Rubery Owen Holdings Limited, for writing the Foreword to this book. His father played a key role in my narrative.

I am grateful also to Sir Stirling Moss, OBE, and to Phil Hill who gave me their time to explain 'how it really was'!

Invaluable advice and assistance has come from numerous sources and I am indebted to them all:

Bob Dance, formerly chief mechanic Team Lotus
Alec Stokes, formerly transmission specialist, BRM
Richard Attwood, Stuart Davey, Maurice Rowe
Adrian Bromley for use of his father's photographs
Chris Gray for giving me the 'final push'
Jaguar-Daimler Heritage Trust
James Beckett of the British Racing Drivers' Club
The Goodwood Estate Co Limited
Automobile Club de l'Ouest
Roger Brockbank for permission to reproduce his father's cartoons on pages 43 and 44

I am grateful to the following for providing additional information for this new edition: Bjorn Kjer (Denmark), Mark Hollman (New Zealand), Nick Loudon and Neil Corner. Also Tony Willis of The Maranello Concessionaires Archive.

My stepdaughter Margaret Finlow, and her partner Andrew Salvidge, for setting up the PC and for patiently resolving numerous crises. Rod Grainger at Veloce Publishing for recognising an idea and allowing it to grow unhindered, and to Judith Brooks and all the team for support in producing a worthy finished volume, especially David Potter who did the book's layout.

Anthony Carter
Wisbech, England

Bibliography

To have witnessed the events one is writing about is a singular advantage but, where memory and diaries have required prompting after so many years, I have had recourse to excellent works of reference, and in particular acknowledge the following:

Bits and Pieces – Being Motor Racing Recollections. Prince Birabongse of Thailand (1942), GT Foulis & Co Limited.
Juan Manuel Fangio – World Champion. Günther Molter (1956), GT Foulis & Co Limited.
Alf Francis – Racing Mechanic. Alf Francis & Peter Lewis (1957), GT Foulis & Co Limited.
All But My Life Stirling Moss Face-to-Face with Ken Purdy (1963), William Kimber and Company Limited.
The Penguin Brockbank. (1963), Penguin Books Limited.
Jim Clark – Portrait of a Great Driver. Graham Gauld (1968), Paul Hamlyn.
Grand Prix Ferrari. Anthony Pritchard (1974), Robert Hale & Company.
Vanwall – The story of Tony Vandervell and his racing cars. Denis Jenkinson & Cyril Posthumus (1975), Patrick Stephens Limited.
Ferrari – the Grand Prix Cars. Alan Henry (1984), Hazleton Publishing.
Colin Chapman – The Man and his Cars. Gerard ('Jabby') Crombac (1986), Patrick Stephens Limited.
It was fun! My fifty years of high performance. Tony Rudd (1993), Patrick Stephens Limited.
BRM – The Saga of British Racing Motors (Vol 1 1994 & Vol 2 2003). Doug Nye with Tony Rudd, MRP Publishing Limited.
Grand Prix Data Book 1997. David Hayhoe & David Holland (1996), Duke Marketing Limited.
Lotus 49 – The Story of a Legend. Michael Oliver (1999), Veloce Publishing Limited.
Airfield Focus No 63: Podington. John Smith (2003), GMS Enterprises.
Contemporary *Motor Sport* magazines and press cuttings.
Amateur Photographer magazine.

Also the following in preparation of this new edition:

Stirling Moss – The Authorised Biography. Robert Edwards (2001), Cassell & Co.
Maserati Tipo 151 - The Last Monster from Modena. Michel Bollée & Willem Oosthoek (2006), Own publication.

Foreword

It is a privilege to write this Foreword because the author has completely caught the spirit of the 'lost era' of motor racing in the 1950s and 1960s, both in his writing and his perceptive and informal photography. We are roughly the same age and both did our National Service at the same time, which made some of those visits to Goodwood and Silverstone so special for me as a fellow enthusiast.

It is always interesting to hear someone else's story of BRM and to be able to say "I was there, too". I remember particularly Fangio's and Gonzalez' first visit to Folkingham to try out the Mark 1 V16 BRM. Fangio drove it like nobody else and, due to the bhp being even greater than that of the Alfa Romeo type 159, could not wait to be on the race track. It did not matter to him that, due to the change to Formula 2 cars for the Grand Prix World Championship, it would only take part in Formula Libre races in 1952 and 1953. I think for the skills of a master driver it was the challenge of taming this most temperamental, all-powerful and difficult car, that must have excited him, together with the scream of its high pitched exhaust. In these Formula Libre races other great drivers such as Farina, Taruffi and Villoresi, and our own Mike Hawthorn, drove the 4.5 litre Ferrari 'Thin Wall Special', and even Ascari in an 'official' works Ferrari at Albi, which gave an additional two to three years in which to see these wonderful cars in action – certainly the crowds flocked to see them.

I did not meet Fangio again until he came over and attended a special gala dinner at the Albany Hotel, Birmingham to commemorate the first British International Motor Show to be held at the NEC in Birmingham in the autumn of 1978. He was seated at the top table with his interpreter and other famous names from the motor industry. During the customary after dinner coffee interval before the speeches I plucked up the courage to go to the top table to speak to him. I explained to his interpreter that my father was Alfred Owen of BRM, and how much I appreciated his driving the BRM. He got up with his face wreathed in smiles, shook me warmly by the hand and said how much he relished driving the BRM all those years ago.

The author remembers well the heady days of rivalry between my father and Tony Vandervell. They had known each other for many years as both ran major private family component companies serving the motor industry. I know my father was disappointed that, in frustration, Vandervell left the original BRM Trust, which had been so brilliantly conceived by Raymond Mays, but there was irony in the fact that it was Vandervell's rival 4.5 litre Ferrari 'Thin Wall Special' that gave my father the opportunity to prove the V16 could win races against the 'Thin Wall'. This also enabled the BRM team to develop the very successful Mark II V16 version so memorably driven by the young Peter Collins in some of the 1954 and 1955 Formula Libre races. The motoring press revelled in this rivalry; a fact not lost on either of them, because it brought in the crowds and many organisers wanted to promote Formula Libre races during that 1952/53 period, even stretching into 1954 and 1955. I remember after one of the practice sessions for one of the Formula Libre races, Tony Vandervell invited my father to see him at the garage where the Ferrari was being prepared. It was 'Alfred' this and 'Alfred' that, and I am sure the talk was still how to bring the UK to the forefront of Formula 1 Grand Prix racing as both at that time were developing new 2.5 litre cars.

The new 2.5 litre Vanwall, coupled with the superb driving of Stirling Moss and Tony Brooks, won the Constructor's Championship in 1958, which only made my father even more determined to win both World Constructor's and Driver's titles with an all-British car driven by a British driver. The Good Book says in Matthew's Gospel: "He that turneth his hand to the plough does not look back" and I remember my father citing this to me whilst driving his Bentley during one of our journeys together, when people began to question whether BRM was ever going to make it.

I remember, too, Tony Rudd recalling he had to make sure that the 1962 BRM car was built with all British made components and, in Graham Hill, we had a driver continually growing in stature. We had come full circle, for the original BRM Trust had set out in 1947 to build an all-British Formula 1 car, to win the 'new' Formula 1 Grand Prix Constructor's Championship, which finally happened in 1962 when an all-British combination of car and driver won both titles together for the first time for BRM and Graham Hill.

The author weaves this story into a most readable and interesting book on an era of motor racing still celebrated by the Historic Grand Prix Driver's Association, and the splendidly revived Goodwood circuit. Long may enthusiasts be the backbone and support for making Grand Prix motor racing achievements so exciting and worthwhile, and continue to celebrate particularly the British achievements of Vanwall, Cooper, BRM, Lotus, Tyrrell, McLaren and Williams, and many others who have graced the starting grids of the Grand Prix scene.

A. David Owen, OBE
Chairman, Rubery Owen Holdings Limited
Darlaston, England

THE Fifties

Early days

Surprisingly, I can remember almost to the day when I first developed a passion for motor racing. As a young lad I was at school near Stamford in Lincolnshire in the early 1950s, and sometimes across the cricket field there came the distant sound of what we were soon to realise was a BRM V16 being tested on the old wartime airfield at Folkingham, a few miles north of the team's base at Bourne. It was a good many miles from us but that unmistakeable whine, ebbing and flowing across the English countryside on a summer's afternoon, had a faintly eerie, captivating aura. It struck a chord and I wanted to know more.

Eventually I came to follow BRM's fortunes through good times and bad, almost as though I was a part of them. Its drivers were the aces of the day; Fangio, Gonzalez, Hawthorn, and others in the early years, all took their turn. It was not until 1959 that Jo Bonnier at last won a World Championship race for BRM after so many struggles – the Dutch Grand Prix at Zandvoort.

In the final year of my schooling, a hard core of like-minded friends and I organised a coach trip to Silverstone with the reluctant blessing of the headmaster, who doubtless thought our studies in that crucial year were of far greater importance than the *Daily Express* Trophy Meeting, 1954. We had the frustrating experience of listening to the first race on the coach's radio as we sat in an endless queue of traffic in the narrow approach lanes in the pouring rain. Admission for a car, driver and all passengers was 30/- (£1.50)!

Eventually we lined up at Copse Corner just in time for the Unlimited Sports Car Race, the drivers sprinting across the road and jumping into their cars arranged in herringbone fashion in front of the pits. Froilan Gonzalez accelerating down the track towards us ahead of the field presented a frightening spectacle, the 4.9 litre Ferrari 375 slipping and sliding on the wet surface as the "Pampas Bull" fought to retain control through the corner. Later in the day our hero, Stirling Moss, was driving the new Maserati 250F which his father had acquired for him in a desperate attempt to give his son a competitive car. Mechanic Alf Francis supervised the construction of the car at Modena and the previous weekend Stirling had bedded things in at a minor race at Bordeaux. Sadly, he had to retire the car from the Trophy race but my first motor racing photograph – unfortunately, a high-speed blur unsuitable for reproduction here – was of Stirling approaching Maggots Curve. Gonzalez won that race in Ferrari's Formula 1 car – the type 625.

It was two years before I got to my next race, but it was a quantum leap: the German Grand Prix at the Nürburgring. I was doing National Service with the Army in BAOR (British Army of the Rhine) at the time, and with a friend took the train from Bielefeld, via Cologne and Remagen to Adenau, a small town out in the country halfway round the old fourteen-and-a-half mile circuit deep in the Eifel mountains. For the Saturday practice we set out on the long walk to the starting area. The race was an annual jamboree for around a quarter of a million Germans who flocked to the Eifel and were already setting up camp on the hillsides. Campfires and cooking aromas pervaded the atmosphere as low cloud flecked the tree tops in the misty air, but nothing was going to dampen the mood of this great occasion. Eventually we were obliged to shelter from the rain as practice continued for the preliminary races, followed by a ghostly quiet of anticipation as we waited for the Formula 1 cars to begin their session.

Fangio's V8 engined Lancia Ferrari D50 burst into view from the distant forest and swept past us at Flugplatz in a great wall of sound. These cars had been handed over to Enzo Ferrari and heavily modified following Lancia's financial constraints, and the death of its lead driver Alberto Ascari at Monza in 1955, ironically whilst testing a Ferrari sports car. We reached the start and finish line in time to see the final lap of a touring car race from the main grandstand opposite the pits.

Something made us turn round; there behind us was Juan Fangio, now dressed in a lounge suit watching the race just as we were. He was unrecognised at that moment and all I had in my pocket was the back of an envelope for his autograph!

The paddock was a relic of prewar days and the mighty Mercedes and Auto Unions – a large paved square for support vehicles surrounded by lock-up garages. We sheltered from the rain in the Maserati garage, noticing Fangio and his wife wandering around under an umbrella, eyeing up the opposition. World champions are made out of such attention to detail!

For the German Grand Prix, we walked in the opposite direction to that of the previous day and made our pitch on the hill leading to the Karussell, one of the circuit's most famous corners.

> "Something made us turn round and there behind us was Juan Fangio ..."
> German GP 1956. The main grandstand outside the Tribune Restaurant of the Sport Hotel (Nürburgring) watching the Touring Car race Saturday afternoon after F1 practice.

Looking across the wooded valley from where we were standing we heard the start of the race over the loudspeakers, followed by an agonising wait before the faint sound of the approaching cars grew ever louder as they weaved their way around the wooded hills. The tension amongst the crowd was almost tangible as we waited for the cars to break cover from the forest. When they did, there was Fangio with Peter Collins and Stirling Moss nipping at his heels shadowing the great Argentinian's every move. The ground fairly shook as they rocketed up the hill in front of us on full throttle towards the Karussell. Fangio went on to win the race and Stirling brought his Maserati 250F home in second place.

Stirling's career had moved on since that wet race at Silverstone two years earlier. Now firmly established as Fangio's leading challenger, he had perfected his craft during the year as Fangio's team-mate at Mercedes-Benz in 1955. Our post race evening was spent enjoying the convivial atmosphere at Adenau's *Wildes Schwein* Inn, evidently the traditional watering-hole for the assembled journalists covering the race. With an interest in journalism I welcomed conversation with W. A. McKenzie, veteran motoring correspondent of the *Daily Telegraph*, and sometimes wonder how my life might have panned out had I followed up that initial contact with "W. A.", as he had suggested ...

Despite heavy heads next morning, we were determined to wring the last drop out of our Nürburgring visit. We came across Peter Collins at a filling station with his Ford Zephyr, only the previous afternoon used to tow his Ferrari out from amongst the trees after the race. He was joined by a car full of Ferrari mechanics and all left in convoy for the return to Modena. Eventually we left Adenau to its sleepy self for another year, walking the last three miles from Bielefeld's railway station to our barracks on the edge of town, falling into bed at three o'clock on Tuesday morning. Like all good soldiers we were dutifully on parade a few hours later!

At the time of that weekend's success, Juan Manuel Fangio was on his way to a fourth world title. It is a sobering thought that he might have remained forever a hero in Argentina but unknown to the rest of the world, racing his home-built Chevrolet Specials in the dusty, dangerous environment that was road racing in South America during the thirties and forties. In 1949 the Automóvil Club Argentino sent the thirty-seven year old to Europe with a new Maserati 4 CLT. He began

winning straight away and was picked by Alfa Romeo for 1950, winning his first World Championship the following year with the updated type 159. Whereas various multi-champions gained their successes with a single marque, Fangio switched teams with ruthless efficiency to ensure he always had the best car to do the job. Thus he went on to win further championships with a combination of Maserati and Mercedes-Benz in 1954, with Mercedes again in 1955, Ferrari in 1956, and finally Maserati in 1957. As he increasingly stamped his authority on the Grand Prix scene, so he found himself competing against much younger aces as the old order stood down in the early fifties. The German Grand Prix of 1957 was surely Fangio's greatest victory, hunting down young guns Peter Collins and Mike Hawthorn after he had been delayed by a lengthy pit stop whilst in the lead. Time and again he broke the lap record, closing on the two Ferrari drivers with frightening inevitability. At the age of forty-six he had driven flat out for three-and-a-half hours, twenty-two laps of the Nürburgring, admitting afterwards that he could never drive like that again. He had taken too many risks. Fangio retired mid-season 1958, forever an admired ambassador for the sport, mesmerising in the cockpit but a shy, quiet man in his private life – Argentina's ultimate champion. His achievement of five World Championships was to stand for nearly fifty years!

Back to civvy street

By now I was in the final months of my National Service, and anyone who has experienced that call to duty will know the only thing that mattered in life was one's demob date! I had a large chart on the inside of my locker door recording the days, and had the satisfaction of progressively putting a large cross through each. I was nearly halted dead in my tracks when, as December 1956 approached, the Suez crisis gathered momentum and we were all supplied with tropical kit and placed on twenty-four hour standby ready to be sent to Egypt. Fortunately, I left the army on time, but saying goodbye to friends I may never see again, deciding what to do with my life, and simply having to organise each day instead of having it done for me presented new challenges, for which many were unprepared.

I had a job lined up as I had no inclination to follow in my parents' footsteps. They were both medical practitioners in rural Northamptonshire, practising long before the days of the National Health Service Act 1948. The surgery, dispensary and waiting room were all part of our house, and private patients were admitted by the front door and offered tea whilst they waited for their appointment in the comfort of an armchair. The other patients waited their turn, knowing they would be seen in due course. My parents ran the practice together, and held four surgeries a day – one at the house and one in the front room of a house in the next village, morning and evening. Their working day (frequently 12 hours) ended at about eight-thirty in the evening, but it was the night calls that would have bothered me most. I would hear the telephone ring, followed by the thump of my father's step on a creaky board outside my room as he went to answer the call. Then a short delay before the front door closed and either my father or mother drove off into the night. It was not unknown for them to return home an hour later, get back into bed and then have a second call out. Maybe that all had something to do with me seeking alternative pastures, I was just too close to the action!

My parents dealt with just about everything. Only the most severe cases were sent to Northampton General Hospital, twelve miles away along country roads. There was no chemist in the village in those days and all medicines were dispensed at the house. It was the job of the gardener to wash out the medicine bottles on delivery from the manufacturer packed in large straw-filled cartons, or on return from the patients. My mother sent out the bills on Sunday afternoons. We sat at opposite ends of the dining room table, me with my homework and my mother with an enormous accounts ledger on her left and a pile of blank bill sheets to her right. How many of these bills were paid I have no idea. The village was at the centre of the boot and shoe industry and times were often hard. It was not unknown for there to be a knock at the door and a brace of pheasants, a rabbit or two, a tray of eggs, or even a joint of meat from a local farmer to be handed over in lieu of payment. During times of rationing this was welcome barter.

My parents were on duty twenty-four hours a day, seven days a week but had a reciprocal arrangement with a neighbouring doctor to take care of any emergency when they were out for their half day. Other calls awaited their return. Even the annual touring holiday abroad was carefully planned and contact addresses and telephone numbers left at home in case of emergency. Arranging for a locum probably caused my father his biggest headache. We had an elderly retainer, but he had the nasty habit of smoking a pipe in bed, which always worried my father. Some years later a distinctly odd character arrived in a dilapidated Ford Prefect. The timepiece which he carried with him was the car's clock on the end of a lengthy winding spindle. Locums always arrived a couple of days early so that my parents could familiarise them with the practice and the needs of particular patients. This man's strange behaviour worried my father so much that he had doubts about leaving him in charge, for maybe three weeks. A series of telephone calls to check his credentials revealed that he had just discharged himself from a mental hospital, so my father had the unpleasant task of asking him to leave immediately.

All this happened the day before our departure for France, and my parents had to make frantic calls to the British Medical Association's offices in London to find a replacement locum. At last one was located in Wales on the point of moving on from a practice, and he promised to come directly to us. He arrived in the gravel driveway in a cloud of dust, which cleared to reveal a handsome prewar Dodge Drophead Coupé. I am sure my father was told but I have no recollection of how this unusual car came to be in our locum's possession. He turned out to be a marvel of a doctor and fully able to plunge himself into the job with the minimum of introduction. However, our worries were not over even then. We were on the point of departing when the springs of the heavily laden 14hp Lea Francis, complete with four people, collapsed as we were driving away! There was nothing for it but to unload the car and drive slowly to the factory in Coventry where staff were on stand-by to perform a swift repair. Somehow we arrived at Dover for a later-than-expected ferry crossing, foregoing an overnight break at Canterbury.

A year or two later my father found a locum who met all his demands and the locum, in turn, liked coming to our house. He was well looked after by two staff who moved in to tend to his every need, and the gardener who drove him around visiting patients; so often locums were left to fend for themselves. Another reason he enjoyed staying with us was the inspection pit in the garage. Our locum friend would spend every free moment underneath his precious 1948 Riley 1.5 litre, lovingly cleaning and oiling the underside and lubricating every nipple. Not many houses would have had such a facility!

The vicar and the doctor were the most prominent people in any village community and, apart from during the war, my father had a new car each year, always the latest model as outward evidence of my parents' success as general practitioners. The range of cars – always two – in the garage over the years would fill a museum today. A bull nose Morris was the first car they had whilst practising in Norfolk during the twenties, but apparently that went through the hedge when my aunt was learning to drive. She never drove again!

The first of my parents' cars that I can remember was a dark

> "The Sunbeam Talbot 90 ... was a fabulous, taut-handling car".

blue Armstrong Siddeley Sixteen-Six, built shortly before the factory switched to producing aero-engines for the war effort. During the war years we also had a Rover 12 with a 1.5 litre engine but, with a heavy body, she was a ponderous old lady. By judicious use of the business petrol allowance we could combine visiting one or two patients with an evening at the cinema, where it was not unknown for the film to be interrupted by a message flashed onto the screen asking my father to go to the Manager's office. This meant leaving in the middle of the performance and returning home as quickly as possible to deal with an emergency. We would drive home in darkness with masked headlamps producing just enough candle power to make out the road ahead. The wide grass verges of country roads were often lined with ammunition dumps – bombs and shells stored under cover of hooped corrugated iron shelters with as much security as was afforded by a tarpaulin sheet hanging at each end to keep out the weather! The ammunition was less vulnerable on these roadside sites prior to distribution to the many airfields in the area.

Mention of those ammunition dumps brings me to the four engined bomber which landed in a large field close to the River Nene two miles from our house. We village lads were on our bikes immediately, our imaginations running riot as we swarmed over the fuselage, taking turns to sit in the cockpit and the gun turrets. Because I wanted to know more about the episode for this story than could be absorbed by an eight year old sixty years ago, I contacted John Smith, a local expert who has researched and documented the history of wartime airfields over a wide area. The problem was that only aircraft which crashed were officially recorded, not those which were undamaged and removed. John has the sort of mind which beavers for information, but even he was becoming pessimistic at ever being able to locate accurate details. My text for this book was almost complete when there came a phone call from John: "I've got some good news for you". What I recalled simply as a four engined bomber was a Boeing B17 'Flying Fortress' nicknamed the 'Monitor' of the 305th Bomb Group of the American Air Force at Chelveston ten miles away.

On 20th March, 1944 the 'Monitor' took off on a mission to bomb a piston ring plant near Frankfurt but was dogged from the outset by faulty navigational equipment and began to lose contact with the main formation in dense cloud over Northern France. There was no alternative but to turn back, an engine failing as they headed for home, dumping the bomb load and all the time losing height. Landmarks could be identified as they followed the Thames and were approaching their base when a second engine failed. Minutes from Chelveston the crew were ordered to brace themselves for an emergency landing, the pilot narrowly missing a church spire before bouncing across a ditch and a hedgerow, landing softly in the field beyond. There were no casualties.

Such was the shortage of B17s that essential repairs were completed on site, new engines fitted, the aircraft lightened and eventually flown out on a temporary runway for the final hop to Chelveston. It would have been pleasing to round off this account with a happy ending but, sadly, it was not to be and the 'Monitor' was lost over Berlin two months later. For me it brought to a conclusion a story which began all those years ago, and for that I am singularly grateful to John and his contact Bill Donald who produced an eyewitness account from the flight's navigator, William J. Rover, to finally set the record straight.

Of cars and cameras

Few cars were built immediately post war because of the shortage of steel and many of these were a continuation of prewar designs. As soon as it was possible however, my father changed the Sixteen-Six for a rakish, powder blue, two door Armstrong Siddeley Hurricane Drophead Coupé, which would have looked at home touring the Côte d'Azur. Later cars I can remember were a 1948 Riley 1.5 (RMA series), similar to our locum's, and also an early rounded-back Standard Vanguard.

The Riley was a gorgeous-looking racy car and its handling a revelation for the time. My mother liked to get her hands on it for afternoon visiting and hustled it through the lanes in great style: I know because I often accompanied her and it was funny how she always managed to find distant patients so as to afford maximum time on the road! There was a Triumph Renown and I often wondered why that handsome razor-edge body design was never repeated except on the smaller Triumph Mayflower. My father was very keen on his Jowett Javelin, a brave new concept, but it had a voracious appetite for gearboxes. Warranty claims eventually crippled the Jowett company.

Later cars I remember best of all – probably because I was at an age to drive them – were the vast, bulbous Humber Super Snipe of the early fifties, a Sunbeam Talbot 90, and a Rover 90. The Snipe was a beautiful car with a 4.0 litre Commer lorry engine; Commer similarly part of the now defunct Rootes Group. It was such a heavy car that it took all day to get up to speed but, once there, it was ideal for cruising along the French *Route Nationals*. I still have a postcard from my father proudly telling me that he had averaged 70mph (113kph) for the first hour along the badly surfaced roads of northern France. Negotiating a humpbacked bridge with that car was like going into orbit, the long bonnet stretching onward and upward! The Sunbeam Talbot 90, and later the sister sports Sunbeam Alpine, was a fabulous, taut-handling car, a joy to drive and proven in rallies with a long record of success in the hands of people like Stirling Moss and Sheila Van Damn.

At the end of my parents' time as GPs in the early sixties, their mode of transport was an MG Magnette with Farina styling, and a Morris Minor, the latter great fun to drive and forerunner of the Mini. After all, Alec Issigonis designed them both!

On completion of my National Service I started work with one of the pillars of the insurance industry in London's Pall Mall. I found digs in Bayswater, a room at the top of a house for which I paid the exorbitant rent of £2-10s-0d per week, or so it seemed early in 1957 when my take-home pay each month was £24-00s-05d.

In those days Bayswater was a shabby and neglected area with just the odd car at the kerbside. One of these was a 1939 1.5 litre SS Jaguar belonging to the owner of the house where I was lodging, and with whom I quickly became friendly once he realised I was a fellow motor racing enthusiast. He used to pop a pint bottle of milk into my room every day and spotted a poster on the wall for the German Grand Prix. That encouraged conversation and soon I was a part of the family, going to motor races in that wonderful motor car of theirs. He had the car tuned by a fellow called Barry who had a workshop in a mews off Westbourne Grove. Barry would take the car out on test along Western Avenue (passing Vandervell Products factory where the Vanwall transporter was frequently seen parked), taking it up to nearly 70mph (113kph), a fair turn of speed for a 1.5 litre car with a heavy four-seater body. Barry had an affinity with that car.

The photographs I took in the 1960s were taken with a straightforward but innovative camera, the Werra, with origins buried in the Cold War. I remember my father being very proud of his prewar German microscope made by Carl Zeiss, which he bought second-hand whilst a medical student at St Mary's Hospital in Paddington. Carl Zeiss was the world's most famous name in optical instruments, and after World War II the factory found itself behind the Iron Curtain, the Russians reputedly sending many of the skilled technicians to factories in the Soviet Union to advance their own optics industry.

Carl Zeiss eventually moved to Western Germany and years later its employees were allowed to return home. Faced with a surfeit of expertise the company decided to enter the economy camera market, the Werra taking its name from the river which flowed through the city of Jena, once home to the company. The Werra appeared on the English market at the end of the fifties and I bought mine from R. G. Lewis in The Strand for about £19, probably in 1961. The 'compact' was sturdy and easy to use, having a 50mm f/2.8 Tessar lens and the luxury of a built-in exposure meter with a selenium cell, thus avoiding the need for a battery. The film was advanced by rotating a collar at the base of the lens through 45° to move the next frame forward, an unusual but utterly dependable system. The fastest shutter speed was 1/500th of a second; no good for motor racing shots which were best left to the magazines. It was paddock photography which interested me most, an area curiously neglected by the three specialist magazines of the time.

Of all the technological goodies we take for granted now, auto-focus is the one I would least want to be without. Trying to focus manually in a crowded paddock, then re-focusing on an invariably moving target, was a constant frustration to that once-in-a-lifetime-shot and must have ruined so many results. The Werra served me well for nearly ten years, using bog-standard black and white Kodak film until the mid-sixties when I was converted to colour transparencies, using 35mm ISO 100 Ilford, and later Agfa film which gave superb results in conjunction, eventually, with a 35mm Olympus 35 RC 'compact'. Sadly, the Werra name was short-lived and disappeared from the UK market in 1966. Today, these cameras command good prices on the enthusiast market.

The negatives I had taken over the years had been boxed up in the loft for decades and it was only when I came to move house – and with the persuasion of my son – that I eventually got around to sorting them out. I had a sample batch of black and white negatives printed 6inx4in and they were a revelation: it was as though I was seeing them for the first time. Another batch followed and then another. Ideas began to flow and that was the beginning of what you see here!

Vanwall versus BRM

I first began buying *Motor Sport* magazine each month as a schoolboy out of my meagre pocket money, and I am buying it still out of my meagre pension! For three decades or more the magazine was largely written by two people: Bill Boddy, its distinguished editor, and Denis Jenkinson. 'Jenks' spent the entire summer abroad, reporting the major races and living a nomadic lifestyle as he roamed Europe in his venerable Porsche, later to progress to one of the new Jaguar E Types. The stories of his travels around Europe often appeared in the magazine.

The first two years of the Formula 1 Driver's World Championship, formed in 1950, were made up of mainly updated prewar cars available at that time, most famously the supercharged 1.5 litre Alfa Romeo 158 which dominated early post war Grand Prix. Dr Giuseppe Farina was the first champion at the age of forty-three and, with team-mate Juan Fangio, shared all the victories that year in their Alfa Romeos. With his relaxed driving style, copied by Stirling Moss, Farina was one of my early heroes – the very name just rolled off the tongue! Sadly, as with so many drivers of the time, his career had been interrupted by the war, and when he got going again he was probably past his best. Farina was a proud man and a ruthless opponent, his face pitted and scarred from the appalling accidents which punctuated his career, largely the result of overdriving. He never again matched his feats of 1950 and died in a road accident in 1966, ironically on his way to the French Grand Prix and long after he had retired.

Although Juan Manuel Fangio was Alfa Romeo's champion in 1951, the writing was on the wall for these elderly cars when Ferrari produced that famous victory by Froilan Gonzalez in the unblown 4.5 litre V12 type 375 at the British Grand Prix. These cars won again in Germany that year with Alberto Ascari and later a resounding first and second at Monza for Ascari and Gonzalez in the penultimate race of the season. Alfa Romeo withdrew its team at the end of the year and now only Ferrari was available with proven cars. Because BRM was still struggling to even start a race with its V16s, the FIA took the decision to adopt the 2 litre Formula 2 for the World Championship 1952/1953, so bringing in a wider range of competitive cars prior to the 2.5 litre Formula 1 of 1954. Thus the BRM V16s, which looked to be really promising for 1952, became obsolete overnight and were relegated to Formula Libre races which catered mostly for out of date cars.

Those of us who were around in those days will have experienced the desperation felt in this country for a Grand Prix victory – any Grand Prix! – by a British car. Nowadays, such a situation seems inconceivable, but in the fifties it was a reality, that is, until Tony Brooks secured that unforgettable win in the Syracuse Grand Prix of 1955 driving a 2.5 litre Connaught B type. The race was a minor event without the presence of the works Ferraris but Brooks defeated the Maserati team and its fancied 250Fs. I can remember the success as if it were yesterday, devouring the newspapers in the NAAFI lounge that October evening. Henry Seagrave had won the last continental Grand Prix with a British car in 1924, a Sunbeam at San Sebastian, and the sense of euphoria at Brooks' victory thirty-one years later was palpable. Sadly, it was an isolated success because of the desperately limited resources of Connaught and lack of competitiveness of fellow British teams. We had world class drivers the likes of Moss, Hawthorn and Collins, but they went off to drive for the Italian teams, so desperate were they for competitive cars! As professional drivers they had to get results.

By this time the Vanwall had emerged. Then called the Vanwall Special, I can remember seeing this strange-looking car,

with its exposed surface radiator, driven by Alan Brown in the International Trophy at Silverstone 1954, one of the early races of the new 2.5 litre formula. The car failed that day but it was the first step on the ladder to eventual success when Stirling Moss and Tony Brooks jointly took a Vanwall to an historic victory in the British Grand Prix at Aintree in 1957, thus beginning the transformation of Great Britain from the role of supporter to leader of the Grand Prix scene over the next decade and beyond.

The Vanwall was born out of the frustrations of its founder, G. A. Vandervell, who had become disillusioned with the chaotic beginnings of the British Motor Racing Research Trust, largely made up of the captains of industry to support and advise on the new BRM project of the late 1940s. Tony Vandervell was impatient for success and eventually decided to go it alone, gaining racing car knowledge and running experience by persuading Enzo Ferrari to sell him one of his latest 4.5 litre Grand Prix cars early in 1951. Vandervell carried a good deal of clout as his company, Vandervell Products Limited, manufactured and supplied the special Thin Wall type big end bearings which Ferrari used in his racing and production car engines.

When the racing formula changed for 1952, Vandervell continued to run his heavily modified Ferrari, renamed the Thin Wall Special, in Formula Libre events in direct competition with the BRM V16s, using ace drivers on a freelance basis. In fact, it was the great Giuseppe Farina, on loan from Ferrari, who recorded the first 100mph (161kph) lap in this very car at Silverstone in 1953. The two millionaire industrialists, Tony Vandervell and Alfred Owen (since late 1952 owner of BRM through his Rubery Owen group of companies), enjoyed the competition between them as their cars did battle in Libre races all over Britain during the following three seasons, Vandervell gaining invaluable working experience for his burgeoning team.

The ugly-looking Vanwall Special that I had seen making its debut in 1954 became a more conventional-looking racing car, the Vanwall, and for 1955 Mike Hawthorn was lured away from Ferrari to lead the team. Sadly, that relationship ended after only three races when Hawthorn parted company with Tony Vandervell after the Belgian Grand Prix, following a succession of car failures, and returned to Ferrari. Suddenly, the whole Vanwall project was floundering with the team withdrawing from the following Dutch Grand Prix due partly to lack of drivers – Ken Wharton having been injured in the other Vanwall at Silverstone in May.

Tony Vandervell was not about to give up and, if mid-1955 was the low point for his team, then 1956 began on a high note with the release of the sensational new Vanwall for which Colin Chapman had been commissioned to redesign the rear suspension and chassis, and aerodynamicist Frank Costin the sleek, long-nosed, high-tailed shape that became synonymous with Vanwall's greatest victories. The first of these new cars appeared in the 1956 non-Championship Silverstone Trophy when Stirling Moss trounced high quality opposition in a one-off drive for the team. Stirling was sufficiently impressed to pin his colours to the Vanwall mast and drive full-time in 1957, along with Tony Brooks and Stuart Lewis-Evans, so building up to that first great World Championship qualifying success at Aintree. Moss won on two more occasions that season, and in 1958 Vanwall scooped the newly devised Constructor's Championship with a total of forty-eight points from six race wins. The Vanwall had at last achieved Tony Vandervell's oft quoted ambition to "beat those bloody red cars", though the Driver's Championship eluded him because Mike Hawthorn, in his Ferrari, defeated Stirling Moss by one point!

Moss' victory in that last Grand Prix of the year at Casablanca was laced with tragedy when Stuart Lewis-Evans, having played a strong supporting role throughout the season, died from severe burns sustained in an accident late in the race. Tony Vandervell was very distressed, feeling that his obsession for racing had resulted in the death of "our brave young friend". He withdrew his team, never again to race for championship honours.

The rivalry between Vanwall and BRM throughout the fifties was intense; a race between two millionaire industrialists to claim success for Great Britain with their respective racing marques. Whilst their aims were similar, the two men were utterly different in character: on the one hand the rumbustious Guy Anthony Vandervell, outspoken and with a fierce hands-on approach to getting things done; on the other the quietly-spoken Methodist lay preacher Alfred George Beech Owen (who never watched his cars racing on a Sunday) who, in 1930 at the age of twenty-one, inherited a family owned industrial empire, Rubery Owen and Company Limited. He laid down the framework of intent for BRM and its execution was left largely to the people at Bourne. That ultimate success was so long in coming was no fault of the indefatigable Alfred Owen.

BRM had to sit out the World Championships of 1952/1953 as it did not have a suitable car. Instead, the V16 was run in Libre events wherever possible to maintain the polish on BRM's racing department and the public's interest and support in readiness for the new 2.5 litre Formula 1 of 1954. True to form, the new car was going through its gestation period throughout that first year, and some doubted whether it would even be ready for 1955! Instead, Alfred Owen made the bold decision to buy a new Maserati 250F, partly so that his designers could familiarise themselves with the new formula cars, but also to keep his drivers in full Grand Prix shape rather than limiting them to the short and infrequent Libre races – largely a UK-based formula. So it was that the Maserati was collected from the factory at Modena late in June 1954 – the price £5200 – and an entry made for the Grand Prix de l'Automobile Club de France a few days later, not for a BRM but a Maserati 250F, an irony that did not go unnoticed ...

Ultimately, the Owen Racing Organisation's first victory in the new formula came with the – by now much modified – Maserati in the 1955 Silverstone International Trophy, driven by a youthful Peter Collins. The all-new, 2.5 litre, 4 cylinder BRM type 25 was at last ready for 1956, having had a couple of tentative but unsuccessful outings at the end of the previous year. Raymond Mays, father of the BRM, and Alfred Owen were desperate to get Stirling Moss' signature on a contract to drive for them, and Stirling was equally anxious to get back into a British car after his tremendous year with Mercedes-Benz. Stirling tested the BRM, the Vanwall and the Connaught at Silverstone on a bleak November day in 1955 and, after much soul-searching, signed for Maserati. The British cars all had huge potential, but needed another year to sort out the 'new car' gremlins.

Finally, BRM's driver line-up for 1956 was made up of Mike Hawthorn, having another crack at driving for Britain, and the inexperienced but naturally talented Tony Brooks. Everything looked set fair for a promising first season with the beautiful type 25, and I held my breath listening on the radio in BAOR to the traditional opening Formula 1 race of the year at the Easter Monday Goodwood meeting. Hawthorn was holding second place to Moss' 250F, but disaster struck when a half shaft seized; the car spun onto the grass verge and was pitched into a terrifying cartwheel with the driver thrown out onto the ploughed infield. Hawthorn was muddied but unbowed and returned to the pits to tell the BRM management exactly what he thought of its new car! It was fast but fragile and failed time and again, culminating in Tony Brooks' fiery accident at Silverstone in the British Grand Prix when a jammed throttle caused him to lose control at the fast Abbey Curve. The car's tail fuel tank was split as it hit the spectator bank and burst into flames. Fortunately, the driver was thrown free and survived with painful but relatively light injuries.

Mike Hawthorn had led the race from the start, both BRMs running in formation – a magnificent sight which everybody feared would not last. Sure enough, Mike slowed and eventually retired with a similar problem to that which had caused his accident at Goodwood, by now utterly disillusioned with both the team and the car. For the second year in succession he was released from a contract while driving a British car.

Alfred Owen was distraught at these failures, refusing to allow the cars to race again until it was proven they could survive a full Grand Prix distance. As a consequence, the cars did not appear again that year and Tony Brooks took up the offer to drive for Tony Vandervell in 1957.

Such were the swings-and-roundabouts fortunes of the two major British teams throughout the fifties. Looking back, it was an extraordinary scenario and British enthusiasts just had to grit their teeth and hope their patience and frustration would one day be rewarded: doubtless the teams shared the same sentiments! The BRMs were on the starting grids in 1957 but lacked a top-line driver. Such drivers were already engaged elsewhere and, more to the point, preferred not to know about poor, struggling BRM.

The team was demoralised and dejected after more failures at Aintree in the British Grand Prix when suddenly, out of the blue, Jean Behra came to its rescue. Frenchman Jean was of the top order of drivers and wanted a car to drive the following weekend in a minor race at Caen in Normandy, where he had the offer of good starting money. The opportunity for founder Raymond Mays and his team was too good to miss and a couple

Jean Behra leaving the paddock in a Ford Prefect, his wife holding aloft her powder compact. His detachable plastic right ear, the result of an earlier injury, was stamped 'Made in England'! Daily Express *International Trophy Meeting, Silverstone 1958.*

of cars were hastily dispatched, the spare eventually being offered to Franco-American Harry Schell, Jean's team-mate at Maserati. Against minimal opposition Jean won the race, dicing with Harry until the latter's car succumbed to engine failure. No matter; BRM had claimed its first important continental victory. It was like manna from heaven for me and supporters everywhere, who just wanted to see the tiniest glimmer of light at the end of the tunnel for this desperately unlucky team. Jean loved the car and the input from a top driver was invaluable. He gave the team the lift it needed.

Six weeks later in September, I was standing at Silverstone's Woodcote Corner on a dreary Saturday afternoon to witness an all-BRM success as Jean Behra, Harry Schell and Ron Flockhart finished first, second and third in Silverstone's postponed International Trophy race – the second victory in a row for this rejuvenated team. There must have been a miracle, or so we thought, as my friends and I happily sat in the traffic queues on our way home. The fact that there were no works-entered Ferraris, Maseratis or even Vanwalls present mattered not at all!

Suddenly, BRM could stand tall and both Jean Behra and Harry Schell had sufficient confidence in the team to sign with it for 1958. Early that year I remember seeing poor Jean crashing into the brick-built chicane at the Easter Goodwood when his brakes failed, then in May at the Trophy meeting, standing at Silverstone's Stowe Corner, watching Jean leading Peter Collins' Ferrari and the rest of the pack down Hanger Straight, only to have a stone shatter a lens of his goggles after eleven laps, forcing him into the pits for attention and to pick up a spare pair. Eventually he finished fourth in a race that he should have won. It sounded like the familiar story again but, whilst BRM was by no means out of the mire, it was on the way to that first championship success at Zandvoort in 1959, ultimately winning the World Championship in 1962 for both driver Graham Hill and the team as constructor. The tragedy was that Jean Behra died in 1959 at the Avus track in Berlin when his privately entered Porsche went over the top of the steep banking. He had given BRM its self-respect and I, for one, felt almost personally indebted to him for that.

We should never underestimate the huge contribution that Sir Alfred Owen (as he became in 1961) made to British motor racing. He rescued BRM from near annihilation, and was tireless in his support over many years when the team was pilloried by the press in a way which is difficult to imagine today. He refused to surrender and BRM went on to flourish throughout the era of the 1.5 litre formula, only to be sidetracked by the complex H16 engine of the 1966 3 litre Formula 1, of which more anon. Failing health obliged Sir Alfred to step down at the end of the decade, the Chairmanship of BRM Limited passing to his brother-in-law Louis Stanley, who also became joint Managing Director with his wife Jean, Sir Alfred's sister. It coincided with the beginnings of sponsorship, the cars no longer entered by the respected Owen Racing Organisation but a succession of title sponsors, beginning with Yardley in 1970.

Successes were few and BRM's last victory came in 1972 at Monaco with the type P160B V12 driven by Jean-Pierre Beltoise. At the end of 1974 the Board of Rubery Owen Holdings Limited reluctantly took the decision to cease all racing activities, faced as it was with spiralling costs and changing times in the group's core industries. Whilst Rubery Owen retained ownership, the staff, facilities and equipment at Bourne were placed at the disposal of the Stanleys who raised their own finance and renamed the team Stanley BRM for 1975.

Sir Alfred's dream of achieving greatness for BRM had been realised. He died in October 1975 and, with hindsight, perhaps the BRM story should have ended there. That was not allowed to happen, however, and Stanley BRM staggered to a painful end with the long-awaited new car (type P207 V12) for 1977 sponsored by Rotary Watches. The car failed to qualify for race after race and shamefully faded away, barely noticed, before the end of the season.

This time there was to be no recovery and it was indeed a sad day in October 1981 when I attended the Christie's auction of the cars and all the assets at Earls Court, London. Even the peeling name board from over the workshop door was for sale! A once proud team which should have become the British equivalent to Ferrari was ignominiously allowed to die ...

Safety? – what's that?

Denis Jenkinson's evocative prose in *Motor Sport* each month nurtured my interest in those early days. Printing schedules meant that reports were often hopelessly out of date when they eventually appeared, and of such length that they ended with odd paragraphs tucked away on obscure pages in ever reducing point size. 'Jenks' caught the atmosphere of the occasion as no other writer before or since, and the more I read the more I wanted to see those great road races.

Meanwhile I listened to BFN (British Forces Network in Germany) whenever possible, and particularly remember the measured tone of Raymond Baxter as he related the unfolding tragedy that was Le Mans 1955. "A pillar of smoke spiralling up into the evening sky"; those words send a chill through me even now. Pierre Levegh's Mercedes-Benz 300SLR flew into the crowd on the pit straight whilst trying to avoid another car and exploded, sections scything through the packed spectator terraces. Eighty-three people died that day in motor racing's worst accident and the repercussions rippled around Europe as governments and motoring organisations reacted in panic. Nobody thought about safety measures; the only way to tackle the issue was to cancel races. Switzerland stopped all circuit motor racing immediately, never to return despite the country having its own Sauber Formula 1 team now and before that, drivers of the calibre of Jo Siffert and Clay Regazzoni. Motor racing was still being run then much as it had been since before the war. Street circuits, public road circuits – just look at the pictures of the fifties and even the sixties and you will see what I mean! The odd straw bale to protect the drivers (or was it to protect the lamppost?), created an even greater hazard: witness the accident involving Lorenzo Bandini in 1967 when his Ferrari rode over a straw bale along the harbour front at Monaco, flipping the car with the driver trapped beneath and the car on fire. Marshals were ill-equipped to deal with the situation and Bandini perished from terrible burns.

Jackie Stewart was the first person to really tackle the safety issue and he had good cause to do so, having been fortunate to survive an appalling accident during the Belgian Grand Prix at Spa-Francorchamps in 1966. The race started in dry conditions but, halfway round the first eight-and-a-half mile lap, the road was awash from rain showers drifting around the Ardennes forests. The drivers were caught unawares and a series of accidents eliminated more than half the field. Stewart's BRM ended up in a ditch, fortunately the right way up, but the driver was trapped and the cockpit filling with petrol from ruptured fuel tanks. It all happened on the long, fast downhill Burnenville Curve and Graham Hill and Bob Bondurant, who had escaped from accidents of their own, ran to assist Jackie. To extricate him they first had to borrow spanners from a spectator to release the steering wheel before they could lift him from the car and get him into an ambulance. Subsequently a spanner was always taped to the steering wheel.

Thereafter Jackie began a crusade to make motor racing a safer sport for everyone involved, from drivers to spectators. The Grand Prix Drivers Association had been formed some years earlier to represent the drivers' views, but it was all a bit half-hearted and lacked proper co-ordination with a central authority: things were very different in those days! Jackie was articulate and commanded attention; in and out of the car his commitment to the sport was absolute. Louis Stanley, whose imposing presence was by then part of the BRM scene, was responsible for setting up the Grand Prix Medical Service as a direct result of Jackie's accident, having been appalled at the lack of adequate medical facilities for the injured driver. It resulted in a fully equipped mobile hospital which attended all the major races and saved lives.

It was a start and the fact that Formula 1 is so safe today is largely due to the vision and determination of such people. It did not meet with unanimous approval and Jackie Stewart and others had their critics, particularly from the press. It was rather like the compulsory wearing of safety belts, it takes time to change public opinion. With ever increasing speeds, it was suggested cars should be suited to the circuits instead of circuits to the cars. Safety is an ever evolving process. Remember catch fencing? Drivers who harmlessly ran out of road into the retarding fences

Patsy Burt returning to the paddock at the Goodwood Festival of Speed 1993 in her unique 4.4 litre Traco Oldsmobile powered McLaren M3A/2. It was built in 1966 specifically for the hill climbs and sprints. Patsy retired from active participation in the sport at the end of 1970. (This information courtesy of Patsy's husband, Ron Smith.)

were all too often finally hit by a flying fence post and the car wrapped in chicken wire! What was once considered a superb safety system seems laughable now.

Triumph and tragedy

It was 1958. I was twenty-one years old and the world's greatest motor race, the *Vingt Quatre Heures du Mans*, was beckoning. In those days you had to do your own advance planning, there was no Page & Moy or package tours to do it for you. Foreign travel was just beginning to get into its stride, and was very different from when I had accompanied my parents on the annual family holiday to France at the beginning of the decade.

I took a train from London's Victoria Station, having pre-booked at a *Pension de Famille* in the centre of Le Mans. I took up my position at about 9 o'clock in the morning for the traditional 4 o'clock start and was grateful when a French family shared their chicken lunch with me. Increasing activity took place from midday onward as the cars were pushed to their allotted starting places. I was pitched deliberately opposite the Ecurie Ecosse Jaguar D Types. The tension mounted as the afternoon wore on and the drivers took up positions opposite their cars. I have a photograph of Stirling Moss walking up the grid to his Aston Martin amid tumultuous applause, a black duffle coat slung across his shoulders and looking every inch a modern gladiator. The traditional Le Mans start is something no one can witness today, having rightly been abandoned long ago. The tangle of cars as they all shot out from their starting positions was a heart-stopping sight, and it is difficult to understand how a major shunt never actually occurred in those initial moments.

Unfortunately, the thing I remember about Le Mans 1958 is the appalling weather and resulting accidents. It rained a little over two hours after the start, shortly after Stirling had retired the leading Aston Martin DBR1/300, and heavy showers continued, on and off, for the rest of the race. It was the year when engine size had been restricted to 3 litres and lap times were well down, even in dry conditions. In truth Aston Martin should have won, but all the factory-entered cars dropped out for one reason or another and it was left to the three year old, privately-entered DB3S of the Whitehead brothers, Peter and Graham, to move up the leader board as others crashed in the dreadful conditions.

They finished in a superb second place – albeit one hundred miles behind the winners Phil Hill and Olivier Gendebien in a works-entered Ferrari V12. The Ecurie Ecosse dream of winning with a Jaguar D Type for the third year running was dashed when both its cars retired in the first thirty minutes! Aston Martin had to wait another year and the Ferrari won due to sheer consistency in appalling conditions, having led for most of the race.

It was late in 1958 when I spotted a job advertisement in *Autosport* from the British Racing and Sports Car Club, which wanted the successful applicant to take charge of organising marshals for the meetings it arranged all over the country, chiefly at Brands Hatch. I went along for an interview with the Secretary of the Club, Nick Syrett, and to my astonishment got the job! The Club had offices on the third floor of a typical turn of the century office building in John Adam Street, just off The Strand in London. Three of us worked there apart from Nick and it was Patsy Burt – then very active driving her Formula 2 Cooper in sprints and hill climbs – who looked after the Club's membership. At the time she was the country's most prominent lady driver, and in 1959 came fourth overall in the British Hill Climb Championship. Her Cooper was looked after by Don Christmas at Rob Walker's Pippbrook Garage in Dorking. Walker was a prominent entrant of cars for numerous drivers and achieved greatness during the Moss period of 1959/1961. He had acquired his wealth as part of the Johnny Walker whisky family and in 1961, for the new 1.5 litre Formula 1, bought a Lotus 18 for Stirling to drive in direct competition with the works-entered cars of Innes Ireland and Jim Clark.

Alf Francis was now Rob Walker's chief mechanic and looked after the cars, together with Tony Cleverly. He was actually Polish, settling in England after serving in the 1st Polish Armoured Division during the war and adopting an English name. He had carved himself a remarkable reputation amongst his peers, particularly from the HWM days of the early fifties when he kept patron John Heath's cars running on a shoestring budget for drivers like Stirling Moss and Lance Macklin. The team had to keep racing wherever possible, eking out a hand-to-mouth existence from the starting money at events all over the Continent.

Don Christmas meticulously prepared Patsy Burt's powder blue Formula 2 Cooper as a sideline to Rob Walker's own cars. Patsy, in turn, was a fastidious owner, which was part of the reason for

her success, and I remember long telephone conversations with Don as she discussed the car. In addition to my duties organising the Club's marshals, I was the youngest person in the office and had the important morning duty of going round to the Trafalgar Café, below Charing Cross station in Villiers Street, to buy coffees and sticky buns.

My first task as 'boss of marshals' was at the 1958 Boxing Day meeting. Inevitably it received a complete 'thumbs down' from my parents who felt I was breaking up the family party, especially as I had to catch a train on Christmas evening to St Pancras in order to meet Patsy Burt the next morning. We met at Hyde Park Corner and she drove me down to Brands Hatch in her powder blue Triumph TR3. On the A20, approaching Swanley we were travelling faster than I had ever done before, and I got out of the car in the paddock feeling I was now part of the motor sport scene!

I was in the paddock reception signing on the marshals and Jean, from the London office, was signing on the drivers. Jean had to put out a repeated announcement over the Tannoy system, "Would Mr Jim Clark please sign on at the Paddock Office". The calls became more and more urgent until finally, "Would Mr Jim Clark come to the Paddock Office immediately, otherwise he will be excluded from the meeting"! A moment later in walked a stocky twenty-two year old, wearing a navy blue blazer and muttering apologies for his late arrival. It was his first appearance this far south and, in the festive atmosphere of clubby Brands, we were wondering what this Scottish farming lad was all about? Certainly, he had acquired something of a reputation in sprints and racing in the north, particularly with a Porsche 1600S and a Jaguar D Type of the Border Reivers, a friend's racing team. Here, he was down to drive one of the new Lotus Elites owned by his farmer friend and mentor Ian Scott-Watson. I remember

watching the furious dice he had with Colin Chapman in another Elite until Chapman finally pipped him on the last lap and Jim finished in a fighting second place. At this point everybody at Brands took notice of the startling new talent they had just seen for the first time.

Ten years on, all but a few months, I was at Brands Hatch once again, this time as a paying spectator for the BOAC 500 miles Sports and Prototypes race. In the late afternoon there came the announcement that Jim Clark had been killed in a minor Formula 2 event at Hockenheim. The crowd as one stood in stunned silence, utter disbelief on their faces. It could not be true! It was – and the motor racing world lost one of its greatest ever champions.

In late January 1959 I remember Nick Syrett returning from lunch one afternoon with an ashen face and a copy of the *Evening News* in his hand. Splashed across the front page was the news of Mike Hawthorn's death as the result of an accident on the Guildford bypass when his Jaguar plunged off the road. Mike was a great buddy of Nick's, who was devastated by the news. Through the open door of his office I saw him sitting at his desk staring into space, unable to grasp what had happened. It was a complete irony: after winning the 1958 World Championship three months earlier – the first British driver to do so – Mike had returned to his home at Farnham in Surrey to announce his retirement from motor racing in order to get married and to run his Tourist Trophy garage business. He was twenty-nine years old ...

The news of Hawthorn's death was a shock for all of us in the office that afternoon. Only a few weeks earlier he had been at Brands Hatch for that Boxing Day event, not to race but to enjoy the company of old friends on a festive occasion. I remember seeing him in the bar long after darkness had fallen on a winter's afternoon, glass in hand and head thrown back with that infectious laughter – my abiding memory of the man.

Largely it was a false image, however! If Stirling Moss was the consummate professional and Peter Collins the golden boy, then Mike Hawthorn was the *enfant terrible* persecuted by an unrelenting press. Early in 1954 questions were asked in the House of Commons concerning Mike's apparent National Service dodging. He was already on deferment (delayed call-up) when he signed to drive for Ferrari for 1953 and he remained in Italy for much of his career, out of reach of the authorities. Ultimately, Fleet Street was silenced when Mike was declared unfit for National Service following an operation at Guy's Hospital for a kidney complaint just days after winning the Spanish Grand Prix in October 1954.

If that laid one ghost to rest, a far more frightening controversy arose when he unwittingly triggered the sequence of events which culminated in the disaster at Le Mans the following year. Although he was absolved of all blame at the official enquiry, not surprisingly the episode left its mark and there emerged a more intense, mature mind increasingly aware of the dangers in continuing to race. Maybe he had become motivated more by the rewards of the sport in order to secure his financial future. Suddenly it was a serious business.

More criticism followed his rapid and unexpected departure from Vanwall, then from BRM – instead choosing a 'safe haven' with Ferrari where he was reasonably assured of a World Championship. At the end of 1958, with the World Championship secured, Hawthorn was left physically and mentally drained, simply going through the motions in the latter stages of the season following the death of his great friend and team-mate Peter Collins at the Nürburgring in August. It spoke volumes for the new-found professionalism of the man that he nevertheless pushed the dominant Vanwall drivers all the way in the last three races that year, finishing second on each occasion. Hawthorn had won only once all season (at Reims) but the points system favoured his more consistent finishing record. That one point advantage was enough to secure the championship ahead of a devastated Stirling Moss who had won four races, the first (Argentina) in Rob Walker's Cooper in the absence of Vanwall. Once again Mike Hawthorn and criticism seemed to be inseparable partners.

I remained with the BRSCC for six months. I had begun to question whether it was such a good idea to make a job out of a passion, added to which I found myself 'on duty' at Brands on Easter Monday 1959, instead of being at the much bigger event at Goodwood which would have been my preference. I could see this conflict of interest reoccurring throughout the season; maybe the sport was best viewed from afar rather than becoming so deeply involved. I went along to see my old insurance manager in Pall Mall and reminded him that he had promised me my job

The author's first motor car in 1958, a prewar Singer Popular.

back if I found my flirtation with the world of motor sport was not for me after all. He looked a bit shocked for a moment but had obviously had a good lunch because he muttered that, if that was the case, I had best start in the Motor Department and thus preserve my love affair with the automobile!

By this time I was in need of transport of my own to get me to the races instead of always hoping for a lift. Sometime previously I had bought a prewar Singer Popular from an office friend for £12-10s-00d, and it gave 500 trouble-free miles before the crown wheel and pinion failed and the car was towed away to the scrap yard. My only real memory of the car is of sustaining a puncture driving south on the A1 in the early hours of one morning with a car full of friends, all of us pie-eyed after a school reunion. Without a jack we were helpless so knocked up the local bobby who, incredibly, helped us out and sent us on our way, quite unperturbed by our inebriated state! That was a long time before the days of responsible driving and today's drink/driving laws.

I had learned a lesson and now wanted something reliable. A motor cycle sounded like a good idea – or so it appeared at the time! I collected my handsome, new two-stroke 199cc Francis Barnett Falcon from a dealer in Great Portland Street, close to Regents Park. An inherent problem with the machine manifested itself within the first two miles when the engine died and I pushed it the rest of the way home to Bayswater. It did not take me long to diagnose the problem, for the single cylinder plug had oiled up. Francis Barnett was part of AMC (Associated Motor Cycles) which included august names such as Matchless, AJS and James. AMC produced its own engine but it was no match for the trusty two-stroke Villiers which Francis Barnett and James had used in the past, and that was the problem. The AMC engine suffered chronic piston slap and at any speed could be heard the constant clatter as the piston rattled against the cylinder bore. This allowed uncombusted mixture to wet the single plug. Straightforward, you may think, except that even the installation of a new engine at the factory in Coventry failed to effect a cure. My solution, borne of experience, was always to have spare plugs with me and I became quite adept at whisking an oiled plug out of a hot engine, fitting a replacement, and being on my way again in a matter of minutes. This problem did not occur as long as the engine was kept revving long and hard, and it ran with the rhythm of a sewing machine on long days riding down to the South of France and back.

One of the perks of working in Pall Mall was to nip across Green Park at lunch time to admire Aston Martin's latest race winner proudly on display at David Brown's showroom in Piccadilly. The winning car would stand in the place normally occupied by a state-of-the-art tractor, and never more poignantly so than Stirling Moss' DBR1/300 after his epic drive to victory forty-eight hours earlier in the 1000 kilometres race at the Nürburgring in June 1959. It looked incongruous, at rest in a smart West End showroom, dirty and streaked with oil like some sleeping giant after battle. The cockpit held that heady bouquet of oil, metal and sweat after almost eight hours of endeavour, the engine barely cold, it seemed.

The tail of the car bore the marks of co-driver Jack Fairman's valiant effort to single-handedly heave the heavy car back onto the road, after an incident in pouring rain during his brief spell at the wheel. In the process he lost what had been a substantial lead. The July *Motor Sport* that year included a dramatic picture of Stirling furiously leaping back into the cockpit at the final pit stop, poor Jack barely out of it and on his feet!

Two weeks later Aston Martin DBR1/300s came first and second at Le Mans in what had been a race of exceptional attrition, with only thirteen cars finishing out of a field of fifty-three starters. Roy Salvadori and Carol Shelby were in the winning car, and with their success came David Brown's greatest sporting achievement after years of disappointment. In addition, his team gained the World Sports Car Championship at the end of a hard fought season.

The fifties were at an end. Motor racing was about to embark on a new and momentous era ...

5th Aug 1956 — The German GP NÜRBURGRING

Fangio's Lancia Ferrari D50 at Flugplatz during Saturday practice. One stands in awe, not just at the achievements of this great champion but also his sheer stamina. At the age of 45 he was at the wheel here for more than 3 1/2 hours, 312 miles (502 km), 22 laps of the unforgiving Nürburgring (with 175 corners to the lap) in a car that handled like a pig compared with modern F1 racers.

"The paddock was a relic of prewar days ...", here seen across the garage roof tops. Post practice, Saturday afternoon.

The Lancia Ferrari D50 of Alfonso de Portago in its paddock garage. Lancia withdrew from Grand Prix racing mid-1955, after which the much modified cars were run by Scuderia Ferrari.

The works-entered, still unpainted, Maserati 150S in which Stirling Moss finished second to Hans Herrmann's Porsche RS in the up to 1.5 litre race for sports racing cars, run over 7 laps prior to the Grand Prix.

Adenau bridge with sports racing cars entering the circuit to drive to the paddock in readiness for Saturday morning's practice.

Horace Gould's converted Bristol coach, still wearing its original "service" colour scheme of green and cream with the added Maserati Trident badge. Horace retired his Maserati 250F on lap 5 of 22 laps.

The Wildes Schwein at Adenau, scene of much post race revelry on Sunday evening.

"... the previous afternoon used to tow his Ferrari out from amongst the trees ...". Peter Collins (centre) having his Ford Zephyr readied in Adenau on Monday morning for the drive back to Italy. Note the prancing horse transfer above the rear bumper.

3rd May 1958 — Daily Express International Trophy SILVERSTONE

The Jaguar 3.4s of Tommy Sopwith and Mike Hawthorn, wreathed in tyre smoke at Stow Corner in their 'fun' duel for the lead during the Saloon car race. On a subsequent lap Sopwith overshot the corner but scrambled round the outside of the wattle fencing to regain the track and catch up with a waiting Mike Hawthorn.

Peter Collins accepts his trophy from Sir Max Aitken, Chairman of the Board, of Beaverbrook Newspapers, for winning the Trophy race in his Ferrari Dino 246. The Daily Express supported the Silverstone 'Internationals' for many years.

Mike Hawthorn accepts his trophy for winning the Saloon car race in his own Jaguar 3.4. At the same time he offered the car for sale: "One careful owner, never raced or rallied!" Behind Sir Max is John Eason-Gibson, Clerk of the Course and Secretary of the BRDC.

BRM's founder, Raymond Mays, consoles Jean Behra (foreground), his face still covered in oil and brake dust. Jean could have won the Trophy race but for a stone shattering a lens of his goggles. He finished fourth after having led comfortably. Long-serving Chief Flag Marshal and Starter, Kenneth Evans, leans on the furled chequered flag.

Mike Hawthorn drove this works Ferrari 3 litre V6 into 3rd place in the sports car race of over 1500cc. At the Easter Goodwood meeting a few weeks earlier, Mike drove the Formula 1 car and Collins this sports racer, then with a 2 litre engine.

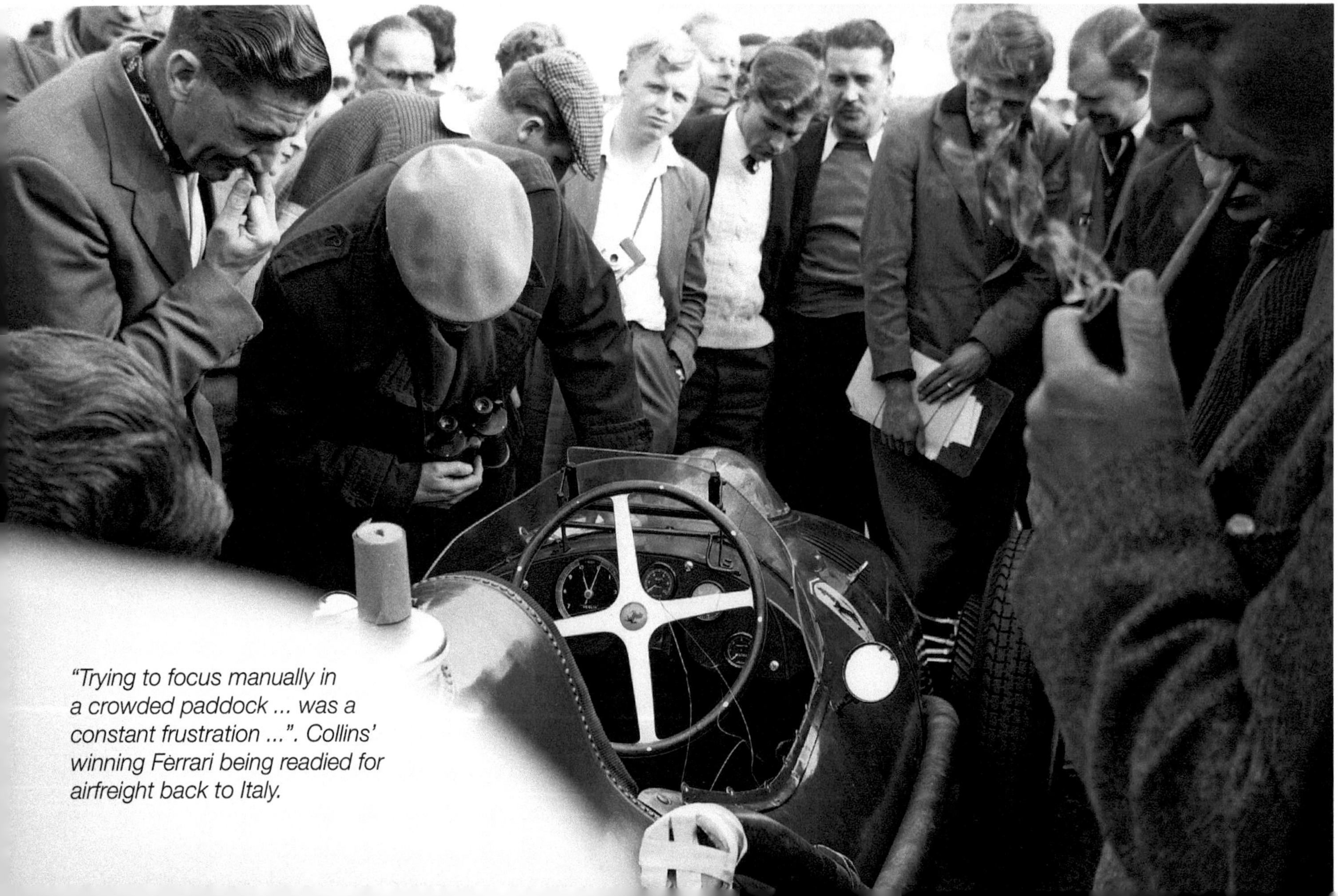

"Trying to focus manually in a crowded paddock ... was a constant frustration ...". Collins' winning Ferrari being readied for airfreight back to Italy.

21-22 Jun 1958 *Vingt Quatre Heures* **LE MANS**

Vintage car parade passing my Pension de Famille in Rue Gougeard, Le Mans.

Dutch-owned Bugattis on display in the centre of Le Mans.

Ferrari Testa Rossa 3 litre V12 of North American Racing Team for Americans Dan Gurney and Peter Kessler. Kessler crashed after Gurney had performed well in his first European race. These 'customer' Testa Rossas with cutaway wings differed from the works cars which had conventional rounded fronts.

Gruber's *famous brasserie and restaurant; always the place to spot 'race people' socialising.*

Stirling Moss watched by Reg Parnell (Team Manager) as he gets into the Aston Martin DBR1/300 at the start of Thursday practice. Behind is the 3 litre Maserati of Jo Bonnier and Francesco Godia. Moss led comfortably but lasted only 2 hours into the race when his engine broke.

Jean Behra in the works Porsche 1600 RSK. A mechanic checks the fuel level with a dipstick. Behra and co-driver Hans Herrmann finished 3rd and won their class. Thursday practice.

The Ecurie Ecosse Jaguar D Types being pushed to their starting positions. No 6 was driven by Jack Fairman and Masten Gregory, and No 7 by Ninian Sanderson and Jock Lawrence. Both cars retired with piston failure after just thirty minutes! Upper engine capacity had been limited to 3 litres to reduce speeds, but caused considerable unreliability when modifying engines.

"... a black duffle coat slung across his shoulders and looking every inch a modern gladiator". Stirling Moss walks up the grid to his Aston Martin.

Gendarmes clear the grid.

The grid in readiness for the drivers to line up opposite. No 9 is the Lister Jaguar of Dubois and Rousselle entered by Equipe Nationale Belge.

Jack Fairman lowers his goggles for the start. To the right of his No 6 Jaguar D Type is chief mechanic Wilkie Wilkinson (hands behind his back). Aston Martin DB3S No 5 was privately entered, and driven by the Whitehead brothers; Peter on the left behind the car. The 3 year old car finished 2nd.

As dusk falls at the Esses, headlights reflect on the damp road surface.

The privately-entered Lister Jaguar of Bruce Halford and Brian Naylor in the pits with gearbox trouble on Sunday morning. They finished 15th. The Jaguars were long gone, enabling the Lister pit to expand!

A chilly Sunday morning as the crowds gather again on the waterlogged terraces to see out the final stages of the endurance classic.

The winning Ferrari Testa Rossa 3 litre with Phil Hill at the wheel and co-driver Olivier Gendebien beside him. They completed 305 laps: 4101.9km at 170.9kph.

The winning Ferrari, all alone at last and showing the signs of having completed more than 2486 miles (4000 km) in appalling weather conditions.

Wet and deserted terraces as chief mechanic Adelmo Marchetti fires up the victorious Ferrari one last time and waits to drive up the ramps of the transporter.

The much travelled Fiat 682 transporter waits for the works Ferraris to be reloaded outside the pits.

This car, in Belgian racing yellow, was driven by Willy Mairesse and Lucien Bianchi but went off in the dreadful conditions. A similar fate eliminated much of the field.

Le Mans went about its normal business throughout the week of the race.

19th July 1958 British Grand Prix SILVERSTONE

Peter Collins with one of the trophies for winning the Grand Prix. John Eason-Gibson is at the microphone, and Earl Howe, president of the BRDC, is to the left with a striped tie. Mike Hawthorn received his own trophy for finishing 2nd – a pint of beer handed to him at a marshal's post on his slowing down lap! Collins and Hawthorn drove Ferrari D246s, as they would at the Nürburgring in the German GP two weeks later. There it was sadly a different story. The debonair Peter went off the road in full view of his pursuing team mate and died from his injuries.

2nd May 1959 *Daily Express* International Trophy SILVERSTONE

Phil Hill's Ferrari D246 loaded ready for Heathrow and the flight back to Italy. Note the high cockpit sides of the 1959 car. Phil finished 4th, the D246 out-classed. Ferrari declined to compete in the British Grand Prix two months later!

THE Sixties

A new era

Just as the fifties were a carry over from the past, going back to before World War II, so the sixties represented a bridge with the future: there were so many milestones which were to shape the sport into what we recognise today.

By 1960 the front engined Grand Prix cars were fading fast, and in 1961 the rout was complete (*) with the introduction of the 1.5 litre Formula 1. Scarab was a new name on the scene in 1960 but too late with a front engined car; a dinosaur before it even turned a wheel. This was the brave enterprise of Lance Raventlow, heir to the Woolworths millions, who wanted to have an American car to take on the Europeans at their own game. As it turned out its sole distinction was to bring the front engined era to a close when a Scarab finished in 10th place, five laps behind the winner in a field of rear engined cars in the last World Championship race of the 2.5 litre formula. Only an aged Maserati 250F was even further behind. It was an all-American story; an American driver (Chuck Daigh) in an American car in the American Grand Prix at Riverside, California.

Along with British racing car manufacturers and probably the bulk of we enthusiasts, the thought of the new 1.5 litre cars for 1961 was utterly uninspiring. It was the smallest unsupercharged Grand Prix engine formula since 1926, and the idea of the engine at the 'wrong' end was complete anathema. For me the most beautiful cars of the previous ten years had been the Maserati 250F and the Ferrari Dino 246. They were every schoolboy's idea of how a racing car should look and sound. Sadly, it was all going to change. The new formula was fiercely resisted by British manufacturers who saw their 2.5 litre cars, with which they had at last achieved success, made redundant overnight. Britain went up a blind alley and prolonged the life of these cars with races under the title 'Intercontinental' as a distraction from the main purpose of Formula 1.

Meanwhile, Enzo Ferrari had long accepted the inevitable and was immediately up and running with an already proven 1.5 litre V6 engine in a passable chassis (the type 156, or 'Shark Nose' as it is best known today). It first appeared in public at the Syracuse Grand Prix 1961, driven by Giancarlo Baghetti, a new kid on the block having his initial Grand Prix outing. They won first time out; if that failed to impress, the same combination won again at Naples a few weeks later. These were non-championship events with incomplete grids but Ferrari swept almost all before it that year, the exceptions being the spectacular triumphs of Moss at Monaco and the Nürburgring when he drove Rob Walker's Lotus 18 with an obsolete 4 cylinder Coventry Climax engine. Phil Hill became America's first World Champion in a tragic race at Monza when team-mate 'Taffy' von Trips was killed after colliding with Jim Clark's Lotus, the Ferrari ploughing into the crowd and killing many spectators. Lessons were slow to be learned; had there not been that terrible accident at Le Mans six years previously? Yet the same sort of thing was happening again with cars colliding and spectators inadequately protected. We may curse the modern debris fence but it is there for good reason.

'Intercontinental' survived only a few races. Britain accepted the inevitable and the beginning of 1962 saw BRM's offering for the new formula; the stunning type 57 with V8 engine and four distinctive upswept 'chimney stack' exhausts emerging from each side of the engine. An amusing cartoon around at the time showed the rear wheels of the BRM digging themselves a hole in the ground under pressure from the exhausts as the other cars raced away from the grid. An early form of downforce, I suppose! For me, the finest cartoonist of the period was Russell Brockbank whose cartoon character 'Major Upset' appeared in *The Motor* (eventually absorbed by *The Autocar*). My father and I made a dash to be the first to laugh at the Major's exploits as soon as the magazine dropped through the letterbox every Wednesday morning. Those cartoons were a hilarious commentary of the time.

Given the maxim that what looks right is right, the 1962 BRM looked a winner from the start, and Graham Hill and team-mate American Richie Ginther went on to have a terrific season, Graham winning the championship against Jim Clark at the final race in South Africa. I remember a BRSCC evening at the Paviours Arms pub in Westminster shortly before that crucial

---

(*) *The notable exception was the Ferguson, a research vehicle exploring the potential of four wheel drive in a racing application. It ran briefly in the British Grand Prix at Aintree 1961, and later that season Stirling Moss scored an important victory with the car in the non-championship Oulton Park Gold Cup run on a wet track where the 4 x 4 concept had the advantage.*

race. Graham and Jim were on hand to give a talk and one sage from the audience asked Graham what his tactics would be right from the start, assuming both were on the front row? With his typically mischievous grin, Graham replied "Cut straight across Jimmy's bows, of course"!

BRM's success that year came in the nick of time because Sir Alfred Owen had made it clear that he needed two victories from his team that season if he was to continue his support. The pay back was abundant, securing both the Driver's and the Constructor's titles, due reward for Sir Alfred's patience and perseverance through those long, dark days when BRM was vilified by the press. The engine, as beautiful a piece of engineering as it was effective on the track, was the work of Peter Berthon whose previous efforts for BRM, particularly the V16, had been notable for their singular lack of success at championship level.

By 1962 the Cooper team was on the ropes, its best days behind it. Charles and his son John forged the team's early reputation, building rear engined cars for what was to become Formula 3, employing 500cc Norton and JAP motor cycle engines in a simple chassis for an immensely popular form of early post war racing. Daredevils back from active service found new excitement, and young stars emerged such as Stirling Moss and Peter Collins. The Coopers decided to build on their success in the junior formula by applying the same rear engined principle to Formula 2 and eventually a Grand Prix design, having a ball before everybody else caught on to the idea. With gritty Australian Jack Brabham's natural engineering flair, they won both the Driver's and Constructor's Championships in 1959 and 1960 before Ferrari spoilt the party in 1961. This was a prelude to the emerging genius of Colin Chapman, who took centre stage and introduced new ideas that raised Grand Prix design to a new level with the 'monocoque' Lotus 25.

The Coopers' fortunes went into decline, unable to match Chapman's wizardry and losing the development skills of Jack Brabham who went off to build his own cars in 1962. There was occasional success, usually with Bruce McLaren before he, too, went on to form his own team. The business was sold in 1965 after Charles died in 1964 and John suffered the lingering effects of a serious road accident with his twin engined Mini Cooper on the Kingston bypass. A brief revival followed under the new 3 litre Formula 1 of 1966, with John Cooper staying on as Technical Director. The engine they were using was an enlarged Maserati V12 which Maserati had developed ten years earlier in the days of the 2.5 litre formula. It was a useful stopgap but the Cooper team was floundering and, by the end of the decade, a name which had changed the direction of the sport had gone.

The Lotus 25 was phased in for the Dutch Grand Prix 1962, Colin Chapman employing aeronautical principles to create a stronger, safer, yet lighter structure which rendered the conventional tubular space frame obsolete. In those early days the monocoque 'tub' was made from riveted aluminium, the box sections containing rubberised fuel tanks which ended behind the driver with a tubular cradle supporting the new Coventry Climax V8 engine. The 'snake pit' exhaust system culminated in a pair of long, horizontal chromed tail pipes, like the barrels of a gun aimed at the opposition behind!

Jim Clark did not win at Zandvoort but did go on to score three victories that year compared with World Champion Graham Hill's four out of a total of nine events. Colin Chapman was not to be denied and, in 1963, his driver brought home convincingly both the Driver's and Constructor's Championships, winning seven out of ten races. After a hesitant start the pessimists were proved wrong and the new formula was alive and well. The cars looked good and those high-revving engines sounded superb.

It was in 1962 at Goodwood on Easter Monday that Stirling Moss had his terrible accident which effectively ended his motor racing career. I was there, standing at the entrance to Lavant Corner, when a cloud of earth flew into the air above the spectators' heads at St Mary's, the previous corner. Stirling had been chasing Graham Hill's BRM for the lead after an early pit stop and, when he failed to follow Graham through on that lap, we feared the worst. My friends and I left the circuit with heavy hearts, having little idea of what had happened other than that Stirling had been removed to hospital in Chichester. Next morning, dramatic pictures of Moss trapped in the banana-shaped wreckage of his car covered the front pages of every newspaper. He slumped there, unconscious in blood-soaked overalls, as he was cut from the tubular chassied Lotus 18/21, a nurse poignantly clasping his hand. Alfred, his father looked on, his face etched with concern for his son's plight, not knowing whether he had a chance of

> " ... return you to the studio".

survival. Had he been in one of the still-to-come monocoques his injuries would have been less severe.

I could never reconcile myself to the fatalities and injury-curtailed careers which were an inevitable part of motor racing in those days. So many of my heroes failed to survive. In 1958 alone five did not make it to the end of the season, and each death was like the loss of a personal friend. Archie Scott-Brown died in a sports car race at Spa Francorchamps; Luigi Musso in the French Grand Prix at Reims; Peter Collins in the German Grand Prix at the Nürburgring; Peter Whitehead in the Tour de France Automobile, and, of course, Stuart Lewis-Evans in the Moroccan Grand Prix at Casablanca. As if that were not enough, Mike Hawthorn died early in 1959. So it continued year on year and, for the most part, it was news that merited little more than a small piece tucked away on an inside page.

With Moss' accident it was different. His was a household name; he was admired by everyone, the archetypal sportsman, the complete professional. The whole world waited ... and waited as he lay in a coma in the Atkinson Morley Hospital until gradually regaining consciousness over a period of several weeks. Recovery from brain damage and other serious injuries continued throughout that summer and, just over a year later, he was ready to step back into a racing car again to determine not only whether he still had the reactions, but also whether he still had the stomach for the racing game.

He tested himself in a Lotus 19 sports racing car amidst great secrecy at Goodwood, as the one thing Stirling did not want was media pressure. Moss came away from Goodwood that day and made the decision to retire from racing. He had set himself an impossible target and when he failed to achieve it he was left with no alternative. It must have been a devastating blow; he was thirty-two years old. The media went into overdrive: the whole world had been waiting and now it had to find a new hero.

Following the races

In the summer of 1962 I went to the French Grand Prix. The circuit, Rouen-les-Essarts, was first used for a World Championship race in 1952 and vied with the ultra-fast circuit at Reims as host to the French Grand Prix throughout the 1950s and 60s. Reims usually won due to generous funding from BP and from the champagne industry, though Rouen was a more varied circuit, similarly made up entirely of public roads and the venue for the Grand Prix that year.

England's circuits were flat, wide and featureless because of their origins as wartime airfields. Whether it was Silverstone, Goodwood or Snetterton they could be inhospitable places, even on a summer's day! Aintree was even worse, its location lacking glamour and atmosphere. Brands Hatch, with its extended circuit, came into the equation in 1964 as an alternative venue for the British Grand Prix. Standing on the infield of the circuit just beyond the bridge after South Bank bend was to see a Grand Prix car in full flight at closer quarters than anywhere, except possibly Monaco. The draught of the car could be felt as it swept by on full throttle, almost seeming about to land in your lap! Silverstone was different with limited viewing and none of the built-up spectator banks and concrete terraces we have today. In the 1950s it was possible to take your car right up to the spectator fence, build a viewing tower from scaffolding poles and sit in a deckchair to watch the racing: today, it would be difficult to recognise Silverstone as an ex-airfield as all that is left is the old Control Tower inside the circuit, used as BRDC offices, and the odd piece of crumbling concrete showing through the tarmac where Wellington bombers once stood. Only the wind and the rain are unchanged ...

I decided to take a longer break than originally intended for the 48th Grand Prix de l'Automobile Club de France. That year there was a non-championship race at Reims the previous weekend which was too good to miss, one of numerous such Formula 1 races that took place in those days. In 1962 there were nine qualifying rounds and another nine international Formula 1 races at Snetterton, Brussels, the Easter Goodwood, Pau, Silverstone Trophy and the Aintree 200, all of which took place before the championship opened at Zandvoort in May. 'Jenks' used to comment that the cars were worn out by that time, but I suppose at least it was useful as a form of early season testing! Add the other races later in the season – such as this one at Reims, at Solitude near Stuttgart, and the Gold Cup at Oulton Park – and it will be seen how hardworked the teams were: a total of eighteen events that year. Many of the top drivers were also competing in Touring Car, GT and Sports/Prototype races such as Le Mans, so perhaps today's stars with their racing and testing schedules are not so overworked after all.

Reims was a tremendously exciting prospect. With generous starting money offered by l'Automobile Club de Champagne, it was certain to attract a strong entry. As it turned out, Ferrari failed to turn up because of industrial strikes in Italy, but the bigger disappointment was that the new works Porsches did not arrive either, Porsche preferring instead to develop its new cars at the Nürburgring after disastrous showings in the early championship races.

I arrived at Reims by train at eight-twenty on the Tuesday evening, having left Victoria at nine o'clock that morning. I stayed at the Youth Hostel in town and caught the flavour of the occasion the very next morning with the unmistakable sound of a BRM V8 hitting the high revs somewhere off the main boulevard. I followed the sound into a side street and found the BRM team occupying space in a garage, along with the Bowmaker Yeoman Racing Team nearby which ran Lola Climax V8 Mk IVs for John Surtees and Roy Salvadori. The wide street provided parking space for the transporters and the support vehicles of Dunlop, busy preparing tyres for the day's practice scheduled to take place between four o'clock and eight o'clock that evening for both Grand Prix and Formula Junior cars. I just stood there and idled away the morning until it was time to begin the long trek out to the circuit. Eventually, I got a lift along the dusty main road in a *Deux Chevaux*, but not before the three BRMs had passed me in crocodile file, followed by the UDT – Laystall Lotuses – all driven by mechanics evidently enjoying taking their charges along the open road and overtaking terrified motorists in a great surge of sound!

I sat and had a much needed drink at the café at the Thillois hairpin, gazing along the seemingly endless N31 Reims-Soissons road, the famous Soissons Straight. It was no wider than the average B road in the UK today, and yet it was here that so many blindingly fast slip-streaming battles were fought over the years. Who can forget Hawthorn beating Fangio (eighteen years his senior) by one second in 1953, or the debut of the Mercedes-Benz W196 'streamliners' in 1954 when Fangio and team-mate Karl Kling played games and crossed the line side-by-side at the finish? Then there was that new boy Giancarlo Baghetti, cheekily beating Dan Gurney's elderly Porsche in 1961 – and so on. Thillois formed a 'V' with another long straight, slightly undulating towards the pits and grandstands, before a series of high speed curves led to Muizon corner at the opposite end of the Soissons Straight.

In the still evening air of first practice it was an extraordinary experience to sit in the tall concrete grandstand opposite the pits, which became an echo chamber as the cars approached from Thillois and passed by absolutely flat, the V8s singing as they disappeared from view beyond the Dunlop Bridge, into the fast right-hander with never a break in the sound! My neighbour glanced across at me, *Gauloise* smoke flowing from pursed lips as he whistled through his teeth. No words were necessary.

It was a different story for the 2.5 litre cars of the old formula. For them on this corner speed had to be checked, and it was Luigi Musso who was caught out in 1958, the car off-line as he lapped another and then lost control. The Ferrari caught the grass verge and flipped, the driver thrown clear as the car somersaulted through the wheat field to destruction. Musso died in hospital. In later years it was suggested he was simply trying too hard in second place to catch Mike Hawthorn and so share the phenomenal prize fund of £10,000 to clear mounting gambling debts. There was little chance of him achieving that because Hawthorn and his Ferrari were at their stunning best that day. It was a terrible blow for Italian motor racing. Alberto Ascari and Eugenio Castellotti were already gone. Italy could ill afford the loss of its last top driver.

That first practice was a case of familiarisation for most drivers, and when Jim Clark turned up late with the Lotus 25 he needed only four laps to beat the likes of Graham Hill in the BRM, who had been thrashing around all evening. When it was all over I hitched a lift back to town in the BRM transporter, leaning against a spare V8 engine, waving to passers-by and thinking that this was definitely a lot better than a day at the office! For the next evening's journey I was promoted to riding in the cab of the Leyland Tiger as the mechanics tore off in their hired cars, obviously anxious to be first into the restaurant. BRM's transporter driver was Len Reedman who also looked after the stores at the races. He was immensely proud of the vehicle, now in its second year, which carried the two race cars plus a spare and all the equipment. A very sophisticated vehicle for its day which cost £7000.

Practice took place over three days with a rest day on Saturday. By Friday I thought it as well to buy my race admission ticket and so avoid a crush at the gates on the day. I found the automobile club's offices on Boulevard de la Paix and fell into conversation with Monsieur Pérouse who, I later found out, was the Président de la Commission Sportive de l'Automobile Club de France. He had gained some notoriety in October 1958 when, as Chairman of the CSI, he announced the new Formula 1 regulations for 1961 to a stunned audience at the RAC Club in Pall Mall. The gathering was there to celebrate Mike Hawthorn's and Tony Vandervell's World Championships, but ended in uproar as the trophy winners looked on in embarrassment. M Pérouse offered me a lift out to the circuit for evening practice, first calling at his home where he introduced me to his family before rushing us off at high speed in his Sunbeam Rapier, of all things, with me holding on to my stomach! Two days later I bumped into him again in the paddock after Sunday's race and he gave me another lift, this time back into town. That was how it was in those days; you automatically felt part of the scene without really trying.

The Grand Prix was preceded by two heats of a Formula Junior race (later Formula 3), and it was then that the day got off to a disastrous start when Bill Moss' Gemini and young Canadian Peter Ryan's Lotus collided at the corner where Luigi Musso had gone off four years earlier. Sadly, Ryan died later from his injuries, cutting short a promising career which almost certainly would have led to Formula 1.

For this big race at Reims in 1962, the front row was made up of Jim Clark, Graham Hill and John Surtees. Any chance of a slip-streaming battle was scuppered right from the start when Surtees went off like a jack rabbit in his Lola, determined to make a clean get away and so avoid anybody latching onto his tail down the long straight. At ten laps he had a twelve second lead, and growing. Then, halfway through the fifty lap race, he was already slowing and eventually retired with engine trouble. Bruce McLaren inherited the lead in his Cooper and went on to win after a spirited dice with Hill in the BRM and Jack Brabham in his Lotus 24 Climax V8 (later in the season he entered his first Brabham Formula 1 car). Nobody begrudged McLaren his success; he was a very popular driver and easy to talk to just like the guy next door. The team he founded remains one of the great success stories in sport. Reims that evening was full of post race activity with the prizegiving at the Hôtel de Ville, a major social event which all drivers were expected to attend.

There were a few days to spare before I was due at Rouen-les-Essarts for first practice the following Thursday. I took an early train back to Paris on Monday morning, noting in my diary that "I had a window seat but it was one of those filthy steam locos"; presumably, the billowing smoke masked my view of the passing countryside. I had a little while to spend in Paris and then on to the Gare St. Lazare for a tedious journey to Honfleur on the Normandy coast. Honfleur was then a quaint, busy little fishing port at the mouth of the River Seine, opposite Le Havre. I say "was" deliberately because it long ago sold its soul to mass tourism, the quaintness scarcely recognisable today beneath the veneer of open air restaurants and cafés, boutiques and ridiculously expensive art galleries.

On the Wednesday afternoon I was off to Rouen, using two country buses which left me with a walk of a couple of kilometres from the River Seine up into the surrounding hills to reach the village of les-Essarts, a few miles south of the city. I remember it was pouring with rain and the only hotel had been taken over by the BRM people, already in residence. Fortunately, Madame at the village café took pity on the bedraggled figure dripping water all over her polished floor and offered me a room, so I was well placed for practice the next morning which began at the uncivilised hour of seven o'clock.

Compared with the impressive facilities at Reims, the main grandstand at Rouen, *'le plus beau circuit de France'*, would have been more in keeping at Mallory Park. The pits were primitive

"... an echo chamber formed as the cars approached from Thillois and passed by absolutely flat, the V8s singing ...".
Grand Prix de Reims (non-championship), 1st July 1962.

and the paddock nothing more than a clearing in the forest! But les-Essarts had one thing that Reims could never match – the gods created this circuit for fifties and sixties motor racing! Set in the chalky, tree-clad hills so typical of Seine et Marne, the essence of Rouen-les-Essarts is best summed up by *Motor Sport's* wonderful cover photograph (August 1957) of Fangio with his Maserati 250F in a full blooded, high speed drift on one of those downward sweeps leading to the Nouveau-Monde hairpin, a scarcely perceptible touch of opposite lock demonstrating his complete mastery of the situation.

To my disgust the Ferraris failed to turn up again and, on race day, I spotted Phil Hill walking down towards the hairpin, keeping an eye on the opposition and frustrated at having nothing to drive. The good news was that the Porsches were there, the team having made excellent use of a break from racing to improve its interesting new car. Porsche had had a difficult first year in Formula 1, 1961, relying on the modified, bulbous Formula 2 chassis whilst work continued on the new type 804. Porsche had developed a flat eight, air cooled engine in 2 litre form and scaled that down to 1.5 litres, but the conventional tubular chassis was already looking dated. The car had a boxy shape, body panels simply covering the 'mechanical bits' with none of the artistry of the Lotus 25. Nevertheless, in its silver livery, it looked good and performed well, Dan Gurney being a surprise winner from consistent running after Jim Clark and Graham Hill had retired. Clark had been experiencing difficulty with the steering of his Lotus for some laps, lost the lead and eventually retired with a defective steering ball joint. I must say the thought of tackling those sweeping downhill curves with dodgy steering is enough to make you blanch: to lose control would almost certainly have involved plunging into the wooded valley below, with not a section of Armco in sight.

The finish of the Grand Prix at Rouen ended in mayhem which, by all normal tenets, should have turned to tragedy. I was watching the race from the top of the embankment overlooking the road just below the start and finish plateau when, suddenly, as the cars were flagged home, there was utter confusion with cars spinning in all directions amidst a great cloud of dust. John Surtees had taken the flag at slow speed, his Lola Climax locked in third gear, and made to turn right into his pit immediately rather than attempting a slowing down lap. The pit lane was barred by a long line of gendarmes, there to prevent a track invasion by the crowd, and they refused to allow Surtees through. Meanwhile, Maurice Trintignant in Rob Walker's Lotus Climax 24 was following close behind and jinked to the left to avoid Surtees' stationary car, straight into the path of Trevor Taylor's Lotus Climax 24 travelling in excess of 120mph (193kph). Taylor stood on the brakes and, with great presence of mind, made an instant decision to hit Trintignant's car fair and square rather than going to the left and risk causing even more mayhem. The two cars were instantly written off, coming to rest at last and the drivers walking away. Incredible! Once again, this high speed sequence of events had horrible similarities with Le Mans 1955 and the wonder is that a car did not land in the grandstand, so close was it to the road. What could have been a disaster was averted by Trevor Taylor's quick thinking.

Poor Trevor, he had the misfortune to be in the same team as Jim Clark in the days when teams could seldom prepare two cars to an equal standard. The result was that Trevor's car invariably suffered, added to which he had some very nasty accidents and, in this particular incident – as with others – he was the innocent party. He was a quick but underrated driver, always in the master's shadow.

Dan Gurney and Swedish team-mate Jo Bonnier, a seldom smiling and serious man, had a famous one, two victory a week later in the Solitude Grand Prix. Thereafter, at the end of the season, Porsche withdrew from Grand Prix racing for reasons which were not adequately explained, and never again graced the stage as a works team. Maybe Porsche expected to 'do a Mercedes' and

win every race but, as it was, its achievement in the first 'proper' year was to finish equal fifth (with Ferrari!) in the Constructor's Championship, one point behind Lola Climax. Gurney was fifth in the Driver's Championship so, overall, Porsche had nothing to be self-conscious about.

Dan Gurney's first season in Grand Prix had been 1959 with Ferrari and he arrived in Europe the crew cut all-American guy; tall, fair and lanky. He became Europeanised as the years went by, an immensely likeable person entirely focused in his work, as quick as Clark in many people's perception. But whereas Clark spent his entire professional career working with Colin Chapman, 'Dan the Man' flitted from team to team, never with the right team at the right time. A few drivers have found themselves in that situation, before and since! Dan had ambitious plans for the future and in 1966 set up his own team, Anglo American Racers, with its own designed car, the Eagle. The project had the misfortune of being two years too early since there was no suitable 'off the shelf' engine available, as would be the case in 1968 with the 'customer' Ford-Cosworth V8 for Ken Tyrrell's new Matra International team. As it was, Dan's decision to go it alone, with Harry Weslake's bespoke V12 from workshops at Rye in Sussex, was probably his undoing, as the whole project was too big and too ambitious.

Dan won the Belgian Grand Prix at Spa Francorchamps with the car in 1967, but that was its crowning glory and the team folded the following year. Dan was not finished, though, eventually returning to the States and building Eagles for Indycar racing with huge success. Now in his seventies, he still seems very active.

I remember an amusing episode at Aintree for the British Grand Prix a couple of weeks after the race at Rouen. The cars were lined up on the grid with the drivers standing around, as they do. Jim Clark (or maybe that wit Graham Hill) had taken

> *Honfleur, at the mouth of the River Seine on the Normandy coast, where the author spent a couple of days 'twixt races' in July 1962. Revisited in 2003, it was found to have "... long ago sold its soul to mass tourism ...".*

Gurney's detached steering wheel and was handing it around the grid as poor Dan conducted a frantic search, moments before they had to get into their cars! And who remembers the words 'Dan Gurney for President' painted on the tarmac at the exit of Druids Hill bend at Brands Hatch? It remained there for years.

Mike Parkes

I often ponder on what it would be that most would call to mind when remembering sixties motor racing. Maybe Jim Clark, Graham Hill and the 1.5 litre formula cars of the first half of the decade, which we instantly recognise, or the GT, Sports and Prototype cars of the era? What is beyond doubt is that the sixties witnessed amazing cars and amazing racing in the latter categories, carried on into the next decade by the battles between the massive Porsche 917 and Ferrari 512S.

If the gods created the circuit at Rouen-les-Essarts, then they also crafted in metal to create the Ferrari 250 GTO which dominated GT racing in 1962/1963. In every curve of its sleek, voluptuous body it was akin to a leopard on wheels, and in England we were treated to regular battles in this category from a number of private owners who entered these beautiful cars. The car was a re-bodied 250 GT Berlinetta which had already acquitted itself with distinction. Whereas the Berlinetta was a very acceptable road car in addition to its competition work, the 250 GTO was undeniably a racer! A solid rear axle and leaf springs were the standards of the day, but the heart of the car was the front engined 3 litre V12.

I was at the Tourist Trophy at Goodwood in August 1962 and the sight of a quartet of those multi-coloured GTOs barrelling into Lavant Corner, then hard on the throttle for the Lavant Straight as all twelve cylinders chimed in, is something I won't easily forget. There was John Surtees in the red Maranello Concessionaires car, Mike Parkes in the dark blue Equipe Endeavour, Innes Ireland in the apple green entry of UDT-Laystall, and Graham Hill in the off-white car of John Coombs. Red really is the only colour for a Ferrari but it must be said that a GTO looked good in any gown. Innes Ireland won the race, but it was John Surtees who led for much of the time until he was involved with Jim Clark's spinning Aston Martin Zagato at Madgwick, so completely wrecking the beautiful Ferrari that it had to be returned to the factory for a re-build.

Mike Parkes was third that day. He was one of the leading exponents of the GTO; in fact, of anything he happened to be driving! A book needs to be written about this man, largely forgotten today, but he was a Ferrari Grand Prix driver in 1966 and 1967 – no mean achievement. He was the son of the Chairman of Alvis and did an engineering apprenticeship with the Rootes Group, being one of the design team of the Hillman Imp. Mike Parkes came into racing with a variety of cars but it was with Tommy Sopwith's Equipe Endeavour that he really came to prominence, driving a Jaguar 3.8 MkII in Production Touring Car races throughout 1961 and 1962. If you study photographs of Mike Parkes, what he did with his cars looks terrifying, yet out of the car he was a gentlemanly person, quietly-spoken and invariably wearing a tweed jacket and suede shoes – long before the days when drivers were obliged to be human billboards wearing their sponsor's gear.

Highly thought of for his GTO exploits, Parkes was noticed by Enzo Ferrari and became one of the works team of Sports/Prototype drivers in 1963. I particularly remember him at Reims that year when he was driving one of the Le Mans 250Ps, fitted with a 4 litre V12 (in place of the 3 litre) in the race for GT, Sports/Prototypes supporting the Grand Prix. He lapped in practice at an identical time with Jim Clark's pole position Lotus 25 – 2 minutes 20.2 seconds – in excess of 130mph (209kph). Admittedly, Clark's car was a mere 1.5 litres but much lighter and more agile than the heavy two-seater prototype. All Parkes' efforts were wasted, though, as he cooked the clutch on the line and partway round a slow first lap he jumped out and pushed the car all the way from the Thillois Hairpin to the pits (or was it just trickling along in first gear with a slipping clutch?), where mechanics were able to work on the car and get him back into the race many laps behind, but at least enabling him to set fastest lap. All this was in defiance of the regulations but Parkes got away with it without penalty: he was nothing if not a tryer!

Halfway through the 1966 season, Parkes was co-opted into the Formula 1 team for the French Grand Prix at Reims and finished second, having replaced John Surtees who had fallen out with the Ferrari management and gone off to drive the works Cooper Maseratis. Parkes was also second at Monza that year and won two non-championship races in 1967, dead heating

with Ludovico Scarfiotti at Syracuse. His short Grand Prix career ended at the Belgian Grand Prix, Spa-Francorchamps in June that year when he lost control of his car on somebody else's dropped oil, the car overturning and throwing the driver onto the road. Mike suffered appalling leg injuries but continued to live in Italy, working at Maranello as an engineer and managing Ferraris for private teams. In 1977 he died in an accident on the *autostrada* near Turin. He was forty-five years of age.

David and Goliath

In 1963, Ford of America had ideas of buying Ferrari to sharpen its image. Crafty Enzo was always pleading poverty, threatening to withdraw his team and abandon racing for good. He took Ford of America to the brink, gambling that outside forces would come to his rescue – as indeed they did – shoring him up for a few more years and thus saving the 'national treasure' once more.

Henry Ford II vowed that if he could not buy Ferrari, then

Mike Parkes! He won three races that day at the International Guards Trophy Meeting at Brands Hatch, 1962: the Peco Trophy for GTs in a Ferrari GTO; the Molyslip Trophy for Saloon cars in a Jaguar 3.8 litre MkII, and finally the Guards Trophy for Sports/Prototypes in a 2.4 litre rear engined Ferrari. The races were run in appalling conditions, and Parkes displayed great skill in adapting from front-engined to rear-engined cars. Performances like these undoubtedly led to Parkes becoming a Ferrari works driver in 1963.

he would beat it! Ford had been chipping away at this task, developing the Ford GT 40 and, eventually, the massive 7 litre V8 push-rod Ford MkII appeared for 1966. Le Mans was Enzo Ferrari's favourite stamping ground: almost claiming it as his own, his cars had won every race, bar one since 1958. Ford knew that to win there would hurt Ferrari more than anything, and a total of eight of Ford's MkIIs were entered by three separate teams, with the best drivers hired to do the job. It was truly a case of America versus Europe, a tremendous battle for prestige. Almost inevitably Ferrari succumbed to the onslaught, and all its works cars were out of the race by early morning. Ford really rubbed Ferrari's nose in it by contriving a near dead heat for the first two cars with the third, whilst several laps behind, backing up the winners by being right on their tails!

It was a humiliating defeat for Ferrari but he came back fighting the next year, 1967. A total of seven 4 litre V12s were entered; three type 330 P4s by the factory, plus another four by 'semi-official' private teams. Likewise, Ford arrived with seven of its 7 litre, push-rod V8s with Ford of America very much in control. Such was the significance of the event that Henry Ford II was in the pits to witness success!

The tension as the four o'clock start approached must have been unbearable. This time it was no pushover for Ford and, whilst it won the race convincingly with A. J. Foyt and Dan Gurney in a MkIV, Ferrari finished strongly in second and third places. Another Ford MkIV was fourth but all the other works and 'semi-official' cars of both teams were out. Ferrari had mirrored the 'David and Goliath' parable, the downtrodden little Italian team waging war against the mighty Americans. Ferrari gained huge kudos as a result, and the crowd made it quite clear who it would have preferred to win!

Ford went home. It had thrown money at the project for the last few years and achieved all it set out to do; the point had been made and the operation was wound up.

Ferrari continued to go about the business of racing: there were more races to win and more to lose. Two years later, in June 1969, Ferrari's future was finally assured in a collaboration with Giovanni Agnelli and Fiat, whereby Enzo Ferrari was to remain in control of his racing team for life with Fiat exercising control over the road cars.

Gas turbine interlude

After the successful Grand Prix chasing of 1962 I was intent on doing more of the same come 1963, but with variations. This time, Le Mans, the Dutch Grand Prix at Zandvoort and the French Grand Prix at Reims all took place on successive weekends in June and these were my targets.

First, though, was the Crystal Palace meeting on Whitsun Bank Holiday Monday. The 'Palace' was always a good place to be on a warm summer's day; what a shame this historic circuit no longer survives. Race meetings there were often organised by the British Automobile Racing Club whose home circuit was Goodwood. The Club moved its 'home' to Thruxton when Goodwood closed its doors to racing in 1966, when it was realised that too much work needed to be done to bring the circuit up to the required safety standards. Thereafter Goodwood was confined largely to a testing role until the Earl of March revived it in 1998 for historic racing. Crystal Palace racing disappeared for much the same reasons; a pity because it was motor racing right there on London's doorstep and so accessible by public transport.

A Formula 1 race was scheduled for that Whitsun meeting 1963 but it never happened, probably due to a shortage of entries since the race was a week after Monaco and less than a week before Spa. Teams just did not have enough time to romp the few laps at this low-key event. However, this did not deter a number of Grand Prix drivers from turning out to take part in other races on the programme. Despite an incredibly busy schedule with the Monaco race, then Indianapolis four days later (where he finished second in Lotus' first foray in the 500 miles classic), Jim Clark was there at the 'Palace' a further four days on to drive a Lotus 23B in the thirty-six lap main event for racing sports cars, which he won. Everything happened in four day cycles in Jim's life, it seems, because in another four days he would be practising at Spa Francorchamps for that weekend's Belgian Grand Prix where, of course, he won as well, so beginning his determined chase for the championship title that year.

Apart from Jim Clark we had Graham Hill, Trevor Taylor, Roy Salvadori and Richie Ginther there that day, all of them top flight drivers. In addition, New Zealanders Chris Amon and Denny Hulme were in the Formula Junior race, still cutting their teeth in the early stages of their European careers.

We enthusiasts had the opportunity of seeing our Grand Prix heroes in all kinds of different roles in those days, be it Jim Clark two wheeling Lotus Cortinas around Brands, Graham Hill and Roy Salvadori in Jaguar saloons, or John Surtees in a Ferrari prototype of Maranello Concessionaires. They, and others besides, were professional drivers but there was another reason for racing in that they were enthusiasts who relished every opportunity to drive anything, anywhere. There was always a new challenge.

There could hardly have been a greater contrast between the tranquillity of a quintessential English race meeting at Crystal Palace and the altogether more highly charged atmosphere of Le Mans a couple of weeks later, where the main focus of attention was the first appearance of a gas turbine powered car. That was as good a reason as any for my being there and I travelled overnight by ferry to Dunkirk, arriving at Le Mans at three-thirty on the Wednesday afternoon of race week, staying at the same *Pension* as before. I was walking out to the circuit along the busy main road through bleak industrial suburbs for Thursday evening's practice, when I managed to get a lift with a marshal in his Renault Dauphine, and he very handily took me straight into the paddock. I sat on the Ferrari pit counter eating my *pain et fromage* as the team's mechanics busily set up their equipment behind me in readiness for the start of practice, all in their familiar berets and brown overalls.

Rover had been pioneering work on a gas turbine project for some years, and the first experimental car, registration number JET 1, now resides in the Science Museum. Rover felt ready to seek a platform to show off this achievement and to distance itself from the dependable, but stuffy image so long associated with 'Auntie' Rover. Even though not eligible for overall placing, Rover was encouraged by the Automobile Club de l'Ouest to compete for a special award of £2000 for the first gas turbine powered car to achieve a minimum distance of 3600 kilometres in 24 hours. Sir Alfred Owen was prevailed upon to burden his BRM team with the task of constructing the car, his design team and craftsmen none too happy at this extra workload when already stretched to the limit defending their 1962 Formula 1 world titles.

However, Sir Alfred's mind was made up. He probably wanted to be in on a little bit of history making and, once agreed, BRM had less than four months to produce a car in readiness for the Le Mans test weekend in April. The concept was fairly straightforward – it had to be with such a tight schedule – BRM simply slicing a redundant Formula 1 chassis down the middle and stretching it in order to accommodate a two-seater sports racer. Not the most attractive of cars, but it had the unusual function of having to accommodate a bulky gas turbine. Regular BRM team drivers Graham Hill and Richie Ginther readily accepted the challenge to drive this unique vehicle.

Standing on the spectator terraces opposite the pits during Friday evening's practice, with the Rover-BRM whooshing its way past lap after lap, I quickly came to the conclusion that I preferred my motor racing served in traditional style with the shrill scream of a V12 in full flight, or the thunderous roar of a V8. That preference was reinforced by the presence of a beautiful and very significant car making a last minute debut – the Lola GT; the Lola with the three-segment Cortina Mk 1 rear lights! A friend and I first set eyes on this car when it was on display at the Racing Car Show at Olympia in January 1963, and we stood there on the stand captivated by its low, silver fibreglass profile. The 4.7 litre Ford V8 engine was mounted amidships and the car looked absolutely ready to go hurtling down the Mulsanne Straight. In reality this was a distant dream as a great deal of development work still had to be done, and the car was delayed on its way to Le Mans by bad weather in the Channel, so that it was too late for pre-race scrutineering on the Wednesday. Scutineering was a day-long affair and, if missed, exclusion from the event usually followed. Fortunately, officials were keen to have this exciting new car compete, and co-operation all round ensured it was on the grid even though a number of last minute changes – such as rear view visibility – had to be made before it complied with regulations.

I was joined by a friend from Jersey on the Friday, and on Saturday we were waiting at the circuit gates long before they opened, a mad scramble then ensuing as all of us there made a dash for the best positions. We were standing right behind Phil Hill for the start. He was driving the factory entered 4 litre Aston Martin 215 Prototype, a very quick car, as were all the Astons entered, although none of them finished the race, unfortunately. Phil's car retired after only two hours, probably due to damage sustained from another car's accident. Through the long night, and indeed for the whole race, we were kept informed by the English commentary provided by the staff of *The Motor* magazine. Even in those days there was a large contingent of British spectators, originating from the interest shown in the Jaguar victories of the 1950s. We bumped into 'Jenks' in the darkness and had a lengthy chat before he wandered off to snatch an hour's rest in his Porsche. Then, during Sunday morning, there was open air Mass on the infield near the Esses with a choir and a sermon in both French and English, although most of it was drowned out by the sound of the cars passing on the other side of the fence only a few metres away!

The Rover-BRM ran like a train that year, 1963, and all the objectives were achieved, the distance target of 3600 kilometres attained with $3\frac{1}{4}$ hours to spare, and finally running into 4173 kilometres, which gave an average speed of 108mph (174kph) for the 24 hours. Overall it was not a good day for the British cars but Rover-BRM would have finished seventh, had it been eligible, behind an all-Ferrari grand slam. The news flashed around the world and I was there witnessing history in the making. Both drivers were incredibly impressed with the 'BRM-like' handling of the car which demanded an entirely different and alien driving technique. The peculiarities of the gas turbine meant there was no engine braking and, at the end of the flat out Mulsanne Straight, the drivers had to lift off and instantly apply hard left foot braking with the engine still driving. Then, say a hundred yards before the corner, the right foot would be back hard on the throttle, still under-braking, to build up the revs again so that the brakes could be released just before the apex, with the engine on full power to launch the car on its way toward Arnage!

Rover-BRM entered Le Mans again in 1964, this time for a placing in the 2 litre class now that an equivalency formula had been offered, but had to withdraw after the April test weekend, partly because the car was damaged in transit returning from France, but also due to engine problems which could not be resolved in the time available. In 1965 the car finished tenth in overall classification, BRM team driver Jackie Stewart now sharing the driving with Graham Hill.

Rover-BRM had achieved the publicity it needed for the project and never returned to Le Mans. The gas turbine idea took off again briefly, this time in a Grand Prix application with Lotus in the 1970s, but it was not competitive.

The Lola GT was driven by Richard Attwood and David Hobbs and performed magnificently in the first hours of the race, though eventually plagued by gearbox trouble which caused Hobbs to bounce off both banks at the Esses at five-thirty in the morning when trying to select third gear. The entire concept was a brave effort from the brilliant mind of Lola's founder Eric Broadley, who operated from small workshops at Bromley in Kent and already had great success in smaller engine capacity classes. This was his first attempt at the big time. As we have seen, Ford of America had designs on Le Mans and joined forces with Broadley to produce what was to become a classic and most successful car, the stunning GT 40. The Lola GT became sidelined and was absorbed into the GT 40 project. Eric Broadley went on to new projects and achieved enormous success later in the 1960s with, for example the Lola T70, a classic in its own right. The Lola GT did not race again as a works effort, and the cars were sold to private owners such as Texan oil millionaire John Mecom for Augie Pabst to drive.

The overall winners that year were Lorenzo Bandini and Ludovico Scarfiotti in the handsome Ferrari 250P, a 3 litre V12, three of which were entered by the Scuderia. They left nothing to chance, even down to carrying rolls of chicken wire in the cockpit to help them out of the protective sandbanks! The winning car was driven slowly past us between the enclosure and the safety bank before thousands of spectators erupted onto the track to share the victorious moments, particularly with the entire Rover-BRM team. The 250P of John Surtees and Willy Mairesse had led for most of the race until Willy took over still with a lead of two laps, and then crashed at the Esses with the car ablaze from a petrol fire after his pit stop. Willy jumped out with his overalls alight, sustaining burns which were to keep him out of racing for some time. Wearily we made our way back into town after spending thirty-three hours at the circuit. Le Mans is a marathon for everybody!

On the road

My friend and I were on a packed train back to Paris next morning at eight-thirty, standing all the way. Then on to the Gare du Nord for a train north east to Senlis, some thirty miles clear of the capital, where we got on to the road hoping for a lift. Unfortunately, we thumbed the wrong guy because, to quote the diary, "… he was a complete madman and drove like hell"! His lorry was loaded with cans of paint which later turned out to be a blessing as he succeeded in running out of fuel not once, not twice, but three times! The first time he replenished his tank from a near-empty can in the back, the second time he ran out of money, and the third time he bartered with a farmer and swapped a can of paint for some diesel! Somehow he got us to the dreary outskirts of Valenciennes from where we caught a tram to the other side of town.

An elderly lady then drove us the remaining distance to the Belgian frontier in "… a clapped out car", returning the way she had come! We walked into Belgium, changed some money and had a coffee before catching a bus to Mons. The Youth Hostel Warden there evidently resented us disturbing his otherwise empty abode that evening, and told us he was closing the door at 10 o'clock in case we were planning a late night out. More to the point, we were kicked out soon after 8 o'clock the next morning and went searching for breakfast in town before walking to the outskirts, hoping to hitch the rest of the way to Amsterdam that day. That was an adventure in itself, which began badly when we found a Catholic priest standing further up the road also thumbing a lift, dressed in his black cassock and beret. With such competition we scruffs did not stand a chance, but fortunately he was on his way quite quickly and we followed soon after in a *Deux Cheveaux*. Later it was a Mini, the crazy driver telling us he had wrecked his two previous Minis, and I must say he gave us no reason to doubt his word! Fortunately, he got us to Brussels intact by midday and then we took a tram to get out of the city and onto the open road bound for Antwerp. The two of us had lots of luck then with a lift from a van, followed by two Volkswagen Beetles which got us to the other side of Rotterdam where an elderly man helped us on our way in his Peugeot 404. He gave us an invitation to join him for dinner but when we realised that he expected certain favours in return we decided to terminate our free ride there and then, and take the train the remaining distance to complete our day's journey.

We found the Youth Hostel at Amsterdam spotless, but 'regulation mad' and were bid sweet dreams over the intercom before soft music lulled us to sleep. Next morning it was jolly music as we leapt from our bunks at 7 o'clock and had the day to explore the delights of the canals and cafés. On the Thursday afternoon we took the train the short distance to Haarlem on the other side of the peninsula, enjoying the more relaxed atmosphere of the Hostel there, and the convenience of a fifteen minutes bus ride to the gates of the circuit at Zandvoort. Here, unusually, we found the paddock barred to the likes of mere enthusiasts and later a policeman pulled us off the boundary fence – all this in pre-Ecclestone days; not what we were used to at all! The paddock photographs I have were taken through or over the fence, which explains their brevity!

If Le Mans 1963 is remembered for the Rover-BRM and the Lola GT, then the Dutch Grand Prix is notable for the ATS, but for rather less worthy reasons. Automobili Turismo e Sport was formed around a number of top Ferrari people after they left Maranello following an internal dispute, particularly Carlo Chiti, the Chief Engineer, and Team Manager Romulo Tavoni. Their new project, aimed at beating Ferrari, was backed by some wealthy Italian businessmen, and they enticed Phil Hill and Giancarlo Baghetti to join them. Both drivers had had a poor 1962 season at Ferrari, so soon after their walkover successes of 1961 which resulted in Phil's World Championship. The problem was that the type 156 was not a match for the British teams in 1962, the flawed chassis no longer disguised by its strong engine. The drivers welcomed the new challenge and I remember the ambitious launch of the ATS when it was shown to the press in December 1962. Sadly, it flattered to deceive. After missing all the early season races, two cars eventually appeared in Belgium for the second championship round and both retired with transmission failure.

The design of the car was along conventional lines of the day, still with a tubular space frame and the driver in a surprisingly upright driving position because the engine was so far forward in the chassis. It was the engine that was the most ambitious part of the project; a 90º V8 with carburettors (fuel injection was still in the future). The concept was enterprising, but the execution abysmal! The whole car looked as though it had been built in a blacksmith's forge and the glum expressions of the drivers said it all. For Phil Hill the ATS experience was the catalyst that brought down the shutters on a brilliant Grand Prix career. After

The author 'on the road' somewhere in Belgium, June 1963.

mechanics went about their routine preparation or unexpected repairs. It should be remembered that at every circuit teams had to ferry their cars to and from the paddock each day, without the luxury of the fully equipped pit garages which teams occupy for the duration today.

Sunday's Grand Prix at Zandvoort was a walkover for Jim Clark and his Lotus 25. He lapped the entire field, a measure of his superiority that year in eventually winning seven out of the ten rounds counting towards the championship. The Lotus 25 monocoque had set a new standard and everybody else had to catch up. Dan Gurney was second in one of Jack Brabham's type BT 7s, and John Surtees third driving the latest type 156 V6 in his first year with Ferrari. Phil Hill spun into the sand when a rear axle stub broke on the ATS, and Giancarlo Baghetti continued for only another two laps in the other car. We watched the race from amongst the sand dunes at Scheivlak, about a third of the way round the circuit, and enjoyed a sunny but breezy day. The thought never occurred to us at the time but, in retrospect, spectator safety was negligible with just a five foot high chicken wire fence between us and the cars – there more to keep the crowds back than to provide any protection.

Phil Hill joined Bruce McLaren at Cooper for 1964 but, by then, Coopers were past their best, and Phil had a fiery accident in the Austrian Grand Prix on the bumpy airfield circuit at Zeltweg from which he was lucky to escape. His confidence was sapped and his Grand Prix career effectively over. I have been a big fan of Phil ever since I saw him win that wet race at Le Mans in 1958, and that same year he helped Mike Hawthorn to win the World Championship with Ferrari. Phil was awesome in Sports/Prototypes with Ferrari and won Le Mans three times. Once his Grand Prix career was at an end he joined American Jim Hall's Chaparral team and I saw him (together with Mike Spence) win the BOAC 500 race at Brands Hatch in 1967 in the 7 litre Chaparral Chevrolet alloy V8 type 2F with the extraordinary driver-operated high wing, the year before wings became *de rigueur* in Grand Prix. I next saw Phil at the Goodwood Festival of Speed in 2001, as keen as ever and driving Chris Rea's replica Ferrari 156. Reminders of 1961 ...

Zandvoort was the first of the 'designer' circuits to be built after the war, the brainchild of Dutchman John Hugenholtz who

another debacle at Zandvoort, ATS withdrew from race after race, the excuse in Germany being that the cars were damaged in transit when the transporter went off the road. Poor Phil Hill, it must have been so frustrating. His best result with the car was 11th place in the Italian Grand Prix at Monza, seven laps behind the winner Jim Clark. ATS disappeared at the end of the season, never to be seen again.

Practice for the Grote Prijs van Nederland 1963 took place with two sessions on Friday and one on Saturday afternoon. Willy Mairesse was out because of the burns he had suffered at Le Mans, and his place alongside John Surtees in the Ferrari team was taken by Ludovico Scarfiotti, having his first Grand Prix drive. Each evening my friend and I went off in search of the teams, scouring every garage in Zandvoort and then looking on as

became much in demand for designing specialist circuits as motor racing moved away from traditional public road courses. Zandvoort's first Grand Prix, in 1948, was won by Prince Bira in a Maserati 4 CLT. 'Bira' was an abbreviation of Prince Birabongse Bhanutej Bhanubandh, nephew of King Chulalongkorn who reigned in Siam (now Thailand) for forty-two years until his death in 1910. Bira came to England before the war to complete his education at Eton and stayed on, drawn to the motor racing game and the society life that was so much a part of it in those days. He returned to racing after hostilities ended and was driving his own Maserati 250F until the mid-1950s. Zandvoort hosted a Formula 1 race every year and was granted World Championship status in 1952 when Alberto Ascari won in the Ferrari type 500 during his onslaught on the championship that year. He won six out of the eight races which, in those days, included the Indianapolis 500. With a few gaps, there was a World Championship round at Zandvoort for more than thirty years, until safety and cries of 'noise' from local residents obliged Formula 1 to abandon it in the mid-1980s. The circuit undulates for 2½ miles through the sand dunes just behind the beaches of the North Sea, right on the edge of the resort of Zandvoort. The disadvantage of this is that the weather is often blustery, blowing sand onto the track, which creates an unusual hazard. It was, and still is, enormously popular for all other kinds of racing throughout the summer and has witnessed significant races over the years, some mentioned in these pages.

Circuit closures are nothing new, and if Zandvoort was one of the early 'designer' circuits, now they are almost universal. I have an old vinyl long-playing record of the 17th Monaco Grand Prix 1959 produced by Stanley Schofield, with a commentary by Nevil Lloyd, and on it is an interview with Phil Hill who was asked for his comments about the circuit. Phil replied: "If it were anywhere other than Monaco it would be scrapped as being out of the question, but it is a little different being where it is". That comment was made nearly half a century ago.

Chaos at Reims

Next morning we were out on the open road once more, this time in reverse direction bound for Reims, where we wanted to be by Wednesday. We had seven different lifts that day and a tram to get us through Rotterdam. Sometimes our lift was only for a few kilometres, one in the perennial Volkswagen Beetle driven by the local priest who took us onto the next village along the way. At the end of the day we got a lift to the centre of Brussels with a friendly Belgian couple in their Borgward Isabella who thought they knew all the short cuts to the Youth Hostel, thus avoiding the busy traffic. As it turned out we felt we knew more about its correct location than they did and, after driving around in circles, pleaded with them to drop us off so that we could make our own way!

On the Tuesday we were off bright and early. Firstly, we took a bus to outer Brussels, then a further ten kilometres in another priest's Beetle and, after a long wait, a run of good luck all the way to Soissons in a Citroën DS 1.9 driven by an Englishman. He had lived in Brussels since the war and had apparently driven an MG to a class victory in the 24 hours race at Spa Francorchamps in 1947. The Citroën DS was unique for its self-levelling suspension but this particular one was being tested to the limit, the boot and the back seat stacked with books. Our driver was a publisher's representative and we sat there submerged beneath the weighty tomes of his stock as the hydropneumatic suspension did its best to soak up the *pavé* and *chausée déformée*. We changed 'lifts' at Soissons for the final run to Reims and checked in once again at the Youth Hostel.

Practice began as usual at Reims on the Wednesday, giving the teams two days to get themselves there from Holland, and to prepare for the 49th Grand Prix de l'Automobile Club de France. This was in complete defiance of FIA ruling which stipulated that there had to be a clear weekend between World Championship races: some things never change! Wednesday's practice was wet, but all day Thursday was a real soaker. I went along and reintroduced myself to M Pérouse and, once again, he gave us the luxury of a lift in his Sunbeam Rapier, this time taking us into the paddock, so saving us the circuit admission charge. It was all the more pleasing to get in free with the collusion of authority! Graham Hill was in BRM's new monocoque designed by Tony Rudd; different from the Lotus 'bath tub' principle in that the BRM was effectively a tube, with just a cockpit opening. The ATS team had withdrawn its entries and returned to Bologna to try to find the horsepower missing at Zandvoort. Instead, Phil Hill was offered a drive in a new Lotus 24 BRM V8 of Scuderia Filipinetti, a major private entrant in those days, generally of Sports and GT cars.

The paddock that day was a quagmire with cars being pushed and towed out of the mud. As so often elsewhere, the paddock here was exactly that; a grassy field with the minimum of facilities, although the well funded Reims circuit was better than most. The pits generally were of the most basic kind – mechanics working in an unprotected pit lane feeling the draught as cars passed by at maximum speed just a few feet away. During night-time racing the risks must have been appalling, but apparently not even considered! During practice days mechanics invariably sat on the grass to grab a sandwich, while the Ferrari team would cook a great cauldron of spaghetti Bolognese on a gas ring ... none of the uncivilised eating habits of the *Inglese* for the mechanics in brown overalls!

A mechanic's lot was invariably unmitigated hard work with long hours, endless travel, and none of the glamour associated with today's technicians/engineers. Dedication must have been a prerequisite to do the job at all. I saw the same people year after year all over Europe, often for a nod or a quick chat as they muttered *scusi* to work on their cars in the open air with a mass of enthusiastic rubber-neckers crowding round. We considered it an absolute effrontery when the more sophisticated teams had an awning mounted on the side of their transporters to give some protection from the weather, and even a rope to keep the crowds at bay! It was comparable to how the fans must feel at being banned from the infield for the Grand Prix at Silverstone: what will it be next?

Although a small independent team, Rob Walker's 'RRC Walker Racing Team' maintained the highest professional standards and the cars were always immaculately turned out, representing a serious challenge to the works teams. At the same time they had style and were out to enjoy themselves. Rob's wife, Betty, would open the boot lid of the Facel Vega (ROB 2) to reveal a wicker picnic hamper, and all would gather round for a gourmet lunch sitting beside the car. Rob was one of life's charming gentlemen, liked and respected wherever he went. I was so pleased at his last great success when Jo Siffert won the British Grand Prix in 1968 in the team's Lotus 49B, beating the two Ferraris. Mind you, I had divided loyalties that day because I would have loved to see Chris Amon's Ferrari win as well, but as it was he chased Siffert all the way, finally beaten by a little over four seconds! Poor Chris, one of the bravest and the fastest, but he never won a World Championship race.

I regretted never having been to one of the 12 hour races at Reims which often accompanied the Grand Prix programme, starting at 10 o'clock on the Saturday evening. There was no such event for 1963, but instead a 25 lap race for Sports/Prototypes and GT cars on Sunday morning. Many of the cars were there from Le Mans two weeks earlier, including Mike Parkes' Ferrari mentioned earlier, the Frenchman Jo Schlesser in the 4 litre Aston Martin 215P and, most enticing of all, perhaps, the monstrous 4.9 litre V8 Maserati 151 coupé entered by Maserati France for veteran André Simon. This car/driver combination had mixed it with the Ferraris at Le Mans and led a good part of the first couple of hours, so was a real challenger here at Reims. It was 'beautifully' ugly, a great single, drainpipe-sized exhaust running below each door causing the ground to shake even on tick over in the paddock. What happened to that car, I wonder?

Saturday was a day for much civic revelry, though I suspect not for the hard-worked mechanics. My companion of the last couple of weeks had to return to Jersey that day, an appalling example of mistiming! In the evening I joined up with a couple of Danish lads I remembered from the previous year, here again for the same purpose as myself. We enjoyed a spot of revelry ourselves that evening, and at midnight drove out to the Circuit in the Danes' ancient and dilapidated Volksbus and completed a lap in seven and a half minutes. Short of walking that must be the slowest lap ever!

The weather was much improved for race day but the Sports/Prototypes and GT event was a bit of a damp squib with the clutch of Mike Parkes' Ferrari failing on the starting line, the big Maserati spinning off early on, and the Aston Martin developing piston ring failure. Italian Carlo Abate won in a glorious 3 litre Ferrari Testa Rossa with Englishman Dick Protheroe a magnificent second in his own specially bodied competition Jaguar E Type, ahead of all the GTOs. Protheroe was a prolific privateer mostly racing Jaguars who, sadly, lost his life in the 1966 Tourist Trophy at Oulton Park driving a Ferrari 330P.

An involuntary pantomime occurred at the start of the Grand Prix. The Race Director was one Raymond Roche, a belligerent and autocratic official, well renowned for fouling up the start of races at Reims. 'Toto', as he was generally known, normally made a point of standing in the middle of the road and dropping the Tricolour to start the Grand Prix, then running for his life – an unwise practice since he was a very large man and the front row was always out to get him! On this particular occasion he added a touch of variety and started the race with a red flag, for some unfathomable reason. Now, we all know what the red flag is for and I have the programme for the 1963 French Grand Prix in front of me which states: 'Signal d'arrêt immédiat et absolu pour toutes les voitures'. I'm no linguist, but I am fairly sure this means 'stop', and it definitely does not mean 'GO'!

To add to the confusion, 'Toto' had already given permission for mechanics to give Graham Hill's BRM a push-start from his position on the front row, just as the seconds were ticking away. It might be said that all but two of the field should have been disqualified instantly for ignoring use of the red flag, the exceptions being Masten Gregory and Phil Hill who stalled their engines and were going nowhere, until that is, the good Raymond quickly conjured up a Supplementary Rule which allowed both cars to be push-started. Then the arguing began!

Eventually pantomime turned to farce as the three cars which were push-started each received a one minute penalty, which seemed grossly unfair since they had acted entirely in accordance with the instructions of the Race Director. Doubtless another Supplementary Rule had been uncovered!

Paddock facilities were primitive everywhere! Here, Ferrari mechanics work on the rear suspension of the Mike Parkes 4 litre type 250P. A white-coated signwriter paints on the number. Mauro Forghieri is on the left of the car. The car was entered for the GT, Sports/Prototypes race prior to the French Grand Prix, Reims, 1963.

The outcome of the race was another convincing win for Jim Clark, but mere results do not tell everything. He certainly built up a substantial lead in the early stages, but then his Coventry Climax V8 failed to produce maximum revs – a singular handicap on the Soissons Straight! Clark was saved by a shower of rain which slowed his pursuers even more than it did him with his sick engine, and he was able to pull away again. Graham Hill was second on the road, but demoted to third as a consequence of the penalty, allowing Rhodesian Cooper driver Tony Maggs to move up into second position. Phil Hill was still running at the end but too far behind to be classified, whilst Masten Gregory retired, thus saving further embarrassment to l'Automobile Club de Champagne!

What fun it all was, spoilt only in that young Scarfiotti crashed badly in practice and injured his legs, leaving John Surtees the sole Ferrari runner, albeit retiring early on. Being back at work the next week seemed terribly dull by comparison!

Dragsters

In September 1964 a different type of motor sport arrived on our shores in the form of American drag racing. The standing quarter mile had long been a challenge, and a number of popular sprints took place around the country, the most prominent of which were the Brighton Speed Trials. We had heard plenty about what Americans got up to in out-and-out dragsters, and the opportunity for the press to see one demonstrated in England arose when Dante Duce made some runs at Silverstone on the Club Straight in 1963. The media interest which followed resulted in the first British Drag Festival in September 1964 on successive days at Blackbushe aerodrome and at Chelveston in Northamptonshire, once home to the 305th Bomb Group and from where, coincidentally, the B17 'Monitor' had originated twenty years earlier.

I was at Chelveston that Sunday afternoon of 20th September to see a handful of American stars such as Don Garlits, Tommy Ivo and Tony Nancy demonstrating their extraordinary 'slingshots', massive supercharged V8 engines punching out nearly 1000bhp on 'dope' fuel. A strong crosswind added a few tenths to their times and the meeting was running late so that dusk was falling as they made their final paired runs, the spectators watching from the other side of a rope barrier. The dragsters were wreathed in tyre smoke as they were launched off the line at ear-splitting revs with exhaust flames stabbing the gathering darkness. It was an unreal, apocalyptic spectacle as they passed in front of us to complete the quarter mile in a little over 8 seconds, a terminal velocity of approximately 190mph (306kph) as parachutes slowed them. The drivers were spinning their wheels for the entire distance, creating a variable gear and thus maintaining maximum power.

Nothing like it had been seen in this country before and, come Easter 1966, the first dragster meeting took place on the main runway of an abandoned wartime airfield on the Northamptonshire/Bedfordshire borders. This was Santa Pod, once Station 109 Podington Airfield, home from 1943-1945 to 3000 men of the 92nd Bombardment Group of the United States 8th Army Air Force. The Group flew 274 missions with its B17s, and 154 aircraft went missing in action. One of the Americans' favourite pubs was the Marquis of Granby at the bottom of the hill where we lived. I would be woken in the early hours of the morning by bawdy singing as they passed our house on their way back to base, two-and-a-half miles away along a lonely country road. Often they were on bicycles, unlit because of blackout restrictions, veering off the road into a ditch, decidedly the worse for wear! Doubtless the next evening they would have been on a bombing raid over Germany.

We local lads explored Podington's abandoned buildings some time after VE Day, May 1945. The mess huts were already showing signs of decay; paper streamers and decorations wafting in the draught from broken windows, discarded 'pin-ups' littering the floor amongst the bird droppings, and the walls daubed with the graffiti of the Americans about to go home. We climbed up the exposed ladder to the top of the water tower, lifted the hatch and clambered down onto the cross beams, peering through the gloom at the lake of murky water below us. Only our bicycles would have betrayed our whereabouts had we failed to return home that afternoon ...

Big bangers

By the mid-sixties I had bought a spanking new 998cc Mini Cooper in red livery with a black roof, suitably 'customised'

> 'Toto' Roche: "... renowned for years for fouling up the start of races at Reims".

from the irresistible attractions of Les Leston's motor accessory emporium in High Holborn. I opted for Microcel bucket seats in black with red piping, a steering column mounted rev counter, a wood-rimmed steering wheel and full four-point safety harness for each front seat. I must say the latter was somewhat anti-social and certainly no good for courting! Profiled wing mirrors and an adhesive number plate on the front of the bonnet completed the 'fitting out'.

A friend of mine had the altogether rarer Mini Cooper 'S' with 1071cc engine, in almond green with white roof, and we frequently went barrelling through the Kentish lanes, presumably in a responsible manner, except, that is, when my friend spun his car right in front of me as we were driving in convoy across the North Downs after a day at Brands Hatch. My car was always a joy to drive apart from an irritating flat spot under hard acceleration, eventually traced to a minute fault in the head gasket.

A friend and I went with the Cooper to the Grosser Preis von Deutschland in August 1965. We stayed in the guest house of the magnificent Romanesque Abbey of Maria Laach, a Benedictine monastery west of Koblenz and well placed for the Nürburgring next day. The Abbot asked if his nephew could accompany us to his first motor race, and late that evening, on our return, we were invited to his study to talk about the day. The Abbot produced a good year's Riesling from within the folds of his habit as he entered the room, and later, when we eventually crept back to our accommodation, I felt somewhat guilty that in a very few hours he would be in the church for Matins ...

We watched the race from Wehrseifen on the descent to the Adenau bridge. The 1.5 litre Grand Prix cars were in their final year before the formula changed and doubled the engine size to 3 litres. Here, the 1.5 litre cars handled like go-karts, the drivers hurling them through the corners, so different from the seemingly ponderous Lancia Ferrari D50s that I had seen here back in the fifties. Jim Clark was electrifying with his Lotus 33 in the race just as he had been in practice and, in fact, throughout the whole season. Graham Hill was second for BRM and Dan Gurney put in a storming drive for third place in the Brabham.

Including Germany, Jim Clark won six World Championship rounds that year, missing Monaco when he was in America winning the Indianapolis 500 instead. He was always the man to beat, giving one hundred per cent every time. His Grand Prix and Indianapolis achievements are well documented: twenty-five Grand Prix victories and World Championships in 1963 and 1965. What have largely receded from memory are his spectacular drives in all manner of cars such as Lotus Cortinas, tiny Lotus 23Bs, Aston Martin Zagatos, and also in rallying. Jim Clark embraced sixties motor racing with an extraordinary natural talent.

Around this period I was watching the many and varied forms of motor sport whenever and wherever I could. If it had four wheels, I wanted to be there! Hill climbing at Prescott, circuit racing at all levels around the country, grass track racing, *Deux Cheveaux* racing in clouds of dust around harvested fields, and the first sight of those strange machines called go-karts. It must have been 1959 or 1960 when Innes Ireland, Stirling Moss and a few of their racing friends showed off the karts to an intrigued public on the infield roads at a Brands Hatch meeting. Little did we realise then that one day Super Karts would be cornering twelve or more abreast at Silverstone's Woodcote Corner in their own Grand Prix, buzzing like a swarm of bees!

Then there were the saloon car races in which Jack Sears first stunned the public at Silverstone in 1963 with the 6.9 litre V8 Ford Galaxie of John Willment Automobiles. That day the all-powerful Jaguar 3.8s were blown away once and for all by raw power as Jack toured round in top gear, having disposed of the opposition on the first lap! To everybody's surprise these American monsters had to be taken seriously, and dominated the category for years.

The big engined, American-inspired two-seater sports racers of the mid-sixties enjoyed a brief but significant interlude. Ultimately Group 7, they looked fearsome and sounded fantastic. One of the first was the Lotus 30 of 1964, a car which Colin Chapman must have wanted to disown, as not even Jim Clark was able to maximise the power in what was an evil, ill-braked chassis. The category flourished, spawning cars from Bruce McLaren's new team and also Eric Broadley's elegant Lola T70, all competing in the Guards Trophy at Brands Hatch and elsewhere, with numerous Grand Prix drivers performing extracurricular duties on their 'off' weekends. Whilst the category raised little interest abroad, it was in the States that these 'big bangers' found their ultimate destiny. The McLaren cars dominated the Can Am series of the late sixties, particularly with the type M8 and its derivatives, Bruce McLaren and Denny Hulme's title-winning performances popularly referred to as the 'Bruce and Denny Show'. Finally, Porsche turbo power took over in 1972, but it had been a significant period in the McLaren team's evolution, ironically marked by Bruce's death at Goodwood in 1970 whilst testing one of his latest Can Am cars.

Unprepared ... again!

As in 1961, in 1966 Britain's Grand Prix teams were largely unprepared for the new 3 litre formula. There was general agreement that doubling the engine size was necessary to re-assert Formula 1's position at the top of the pile, for sheer spectacle seriously threatened by the big engined cars of other categories. Whilst Ferrari had plenty of experience with 3 litre V12s, the major British teams found themselves without an engine when Coventry Climax decided it did not wish to compete in the new formula. Wily Jack Brabham utilised an Australian Repco V8, based on an aluminium Buick engine of uncomplicated design in a straightforward tubular space frame chassis. In the age of the monocoque the car was still good enough to win both championships in a row, in 1966 with Jack and, updated, in 1967 with Denny Hulme, before the rest of the world got its act together and caught up. Cooper had persuaded Maserati back into racing with the supply of the updated V12, but it was underpowered and too heavy. Bruce McLaren was there for 1966, already building successful sports racing cars, using a scaled down 4.2 litre Indianapolis Ford V8 initially, then trying an Italian Serenissima V8, but was having a disastrous first season in Formula 1. He was suffering similar problems to those of Dan Gurney's Eagle team that same year.

Only BRM seemed prepared – on paper, at least. Chief Engineer Tony Rudd was convinced he had achieved optimum performance from the final specification of the successful 1.5 litre V8, and hoped to replicate that by effectively stacking two units, flattened, one above the other to form a 3 litre engine in H16 format with gearing linking the two crankshafts. It was an exciting prospect but the end result was overweight and lacking power: BRM and sixteen cylinders were never intended to be bed fellows! BRM had agreed to supply the engine to its greatest rival – Lotus, but event after event passed in 1966 before it was considered raceworthy.

Meanwhile, both teams had to make do with obsolete cars and engines. The H16 was at last deemed ready for both teams to use at Monza in 1966 but, ironically, it was Jim Clark who achieved the only success for the engine at Watkins Glen in the US Grand Prix, the penultimate race of the season.

Engine supply to Lotus from BRM was only a temporary arrangement pending arrival of the Ford-Cosworth which Ford had agreed to fund to the tune of £100,000, when it was known at the end of 1965 that Coventry Climax was withdrawing. Ford and Lotus had collaborated on various projects throughout the early sixties, notably their success at Indianapolis, and the Cosworth engine supply was an exclusive deal once it was fully tested and ready for 1967. Graham Hill was taken on board to partner Jim Clark, Ford insistent on two top flight drivers to justify its investment, although for Hill it meant breaking his link with BRM, with whom he had become synonymous during their seven great years together. John Surtees went to Honda, having parted company with Cooper. Dan Gurney's Eagles were looking promising and, generally, everybody seemed much better prepared and ready to go for 1967.

The new Ford-Cosworth engine was not delivered in time for the first European race at Monaco but, at Zandvoort a month later, the all-new Lotus 49 Ford-Cosworth V8 was an absolute sensation. Once again Colin Chapman set the standard that others had to follow, the monocoque and the engine designed as an all-in-one combination right from the first line on the drawing board. The monocoque ended behind the cockpit with the engine attached at two points top and bottom to form a fully stressed extension of the car, to which the gearbox and rear suspension were mounted.

Graham Hill put his car on pole and led initially until his new engine failed; thereafter Clark took over and motored off into the distance. Jim Clark won another three races that year, but on sheer consistency Denny Hulme and his boss Jack Brabham took the Driver's (first and second respectively) and Constructor's Championships because of more point scoring finishes.

Maranello

I had been in love with Ferraris from the moment I first saw Froilan Gonzalez grappling with that fearsome brute, the 4.9 litre V12 Ferrari 375 in the wet at Silverstone way back in 1954. When my first wife and I planned a camping trip abroad in 1967 I was determined that Maranello would feature large on the itinerary. I wrote to Colonel Ronnie Hoare, Chairman of Maranello Concessionaires, then at Wellesley Road in Chiswick, and received a charming letter in reply telling me that organised factory visits took place on Saturday afternoons at two o'clock, and would I please give him the preferred date?

So it was that in June that year we set out for Dover in our dark blue Volkswagen 1200 Beetle with a frame tent stacked on the rear seat, and the boot 'up front' packed with all the paraphernalia needed for three weeks abroad. We had decided not to bother with the obligatory yellow head lamps for driving in France, since it would have masked what feeble light there was from the 6 volt battery on that car. When we moved up to a Beetle 1500 a couple of years later we had the luxury of a 12 volt battery, and were thrilled when oncoming drivers flashed us because we were on main beam, something of a novelty even with that car!

We passed through France into Switzerland, spending our first Sunday night camping on a remote hillside site, but with plenty of people about enjoying barbecues in the evening air. When we unzipped our tent flap next morning we found the place utterly deserted. Apparently the weekend campers had returned home, leaving their static tents behind ready for their next visit. We were alone in the mist and eerie silence of the mountains.

From Switzerland we crossed into Italy by the Simplon Pass, eventually arriving at an idyllic campsite at Fiesole on the hill slopes above Florence. The sound of church bells floating on the summer air next morning belied the day seven months earlier when the city was devastated by floods, as the mighty River Arno burst its banks after incessant autumn rains poured off the surrounding hillsides. A huge clean-up operation was in progress everywhere we went. Today, looking up at the flood water level commemorated on a building in the Piazza Duomo, it is difficult to imagine how this Renaissance city recovered from probably greater damage than was inflicted by the German army in 1944 ...

The main focus of our Italian interlude was always going to be Maranello, and, firstly we had to report to the Ferrari Service Centre at Modena, some miles away. Modena was the 'silicone valley' of Italian motor racing in those days, famous as the home of Maserati and all manner of small manufacturers such as de Tomaso and Tec Mec, and various coach-building workshops. It is also another magnificent Renaissance city with its duomo occupying one side of an airy, arcaded cobbled square. The city's charms had to wait for another time, however, and we left our travel-worn Beetle amongst a plethora of customers' exotic Ferraris in various stages of undress awaiting attention!

Our guide must have thought he was going to have the afternoon off because there were no other visitors that day; evidently there had been some communications malfunction as he did not seem to be aware of our impending arrival. We remained undaunted: having got that far there was no way we were going to be turned away! Such a predicament was never going to arise, thankfully, because our guide was charm itself, spoke excellent English, and seemed to revel in having more personal contact with his two visitors than with a large party. We were driven along country roads to Maranello – not in a company Dino 206 GT but a Fiat 125, pressing on in energetic style and taking a racing line through every corner as our guide enquired about our travels.

After parking the car we walked through the hallowed archway above which was Enzo Ferrari's office. Beyond was a large triangular courtyard with, as I recall, factory buildings on three sides and conifers in the centre shielding Shell petrol pumps. The racing workshop on the left really caught my eye because the body panels of a 330 P4 Sports Prototype were standing outside on boxes, having just been sprayed that distinctive shade of Italian racing red, and left to dry in the hot afternoon sunshine.

The workshop was one of the original buildings erected after the war when Ferrari first occupied the site, a single storey, biscuit-coloured building into which I peeped to see various competition cars undergoing preparation. Not surprisingly it was the only sight I had of that part of the factory!

More was to come though as, hidden for the moment by the conifers, was a 330 P4 4 litre V12, minus its front bodywork and destined for Le Mans the next weekend, where it would be on loan to *Equipe Nationale Belge* and driven into third place by Willy Mairesse and 'Beurlys'. The car here that Saturday afternoon had a broad yellow stripe down the centre in recognition of its temporary Belgian ownership, and was receiving a few litres of petrol in readiness for a dozen or so laps of the courtyard. I took a couple of photographs and stood mesmerised as a mechanic climbed aboard and the V12 burst into life to be driven round and round. Our continuing tour of the factory was accompanied by the sounds of great bursts of acceleration followed by savage braking, probably the car's last work-out before despatch to Le Mans. The days of Ferrari's own test track at Fiorano were still in the future. There was an old track at Modena for testing but it seems the courtyard 'test' was how cars were given the final 'OK'.

We could go anywhere and photograph what we wished that Saturday afternoon. We saw the foundry, the engine build shop, and the deserted factory floor where lathes and grinding machines stood idle except for the odd technician working on his own. The pictures elsewhere in this book tell their own story but, unfortunately, I missed taking a photograph of the engine test house. We were shielded in a partially soundproofed ante-room, watching through a heavy glass panel as one of the V12s was put through its paces on the test bed. An engineer monitored a control panel as the engine was held at peak revs (probably in preparation for the Mulsanne Straight!), the exhausts glowing red hot. The sound was shattering, even with soundproofing!

Our guide talked to us all the time, answering our questions and explaining the sense of loss felt around the factory at the death of Lorenzo Bandini in the fiery accident at Monaco only a few weeks earlier. He was thirty-one years of age, Italy's great hope for the future. The evening before the team left for Monaco, Lorenzo and few a friends had dined at the famous *il Cavalino* restaurant opposite the factory gates. Little did they realise that this would be the last they saw of him. He was irreplaceable.

Enzo Ferrari had such a terrible time with press criticism over the loss of his Italian drivers that it was the mid-1980s before another Italian, Michele Alboreto, took a leading role in the team. The lack of Italian drivers in the Ferrari team holds good even in this modern era. The cold hand of tragedy threatened Enzo Ferrari every day of his life; even his son Dino died from an incurable disease whilst still a young man. I have often wondered how one man dealt with the sense of guilt he must have felt at the loss of so many drivers at the wheels of his cars. Alberto Ascari, Eugenio Castelotti, Luigi Musso, Peter Collins and Gilles Villeneuve, to name but a few, all died in a Ferrari racing car. So many lives; so many deaths. Ferrari was a complete enigma, though that he was a tough character is beyond doubt: he had to be! Yet it is for his cars that Enzo Ferrari is always going to be remembered. We all have our particular favourites and for me the GTO is one and the 330 P4 another. The list goes on ... and on!

Endlessly talking about our experiences so far we headed north towards Venice, camping at Lido di Jesolo at the end of the peninsula opposite the city. There was a ferocious thunderstorm that night which nearly brought the tent down, and the next day Venice appeared out of the silvery mist with a haunting, surreal quality as our ferry approached through the calm waters so different from the previous night.

We were continually on the move that year, and barely had time to see the pigeons in St Mark's Square before we were off again the next day across the mountains to Innsbruck, crossing the Brenner Pass and the magnificent *Europabrücke*, recently opened. Onward to Bavaria and Oberammergau, to Rothenburg and the old towns along the *Romantischen Strasse*, then alongside Lake Constance to Freiburg, to Alsace – and the remainder of our journey home in our travel-weary but unfaltering Beetle.

Changing times

It was in 1968 that the face of the sport changed again with the arrival of corporate sponsorship. The days of national racing colours were numbered when the traditional trade backers showed signs of reducing their involvement. Their participation had been discreet; in fact, barely recognised except for post race advertising in newspapers and the specialist press. Now, motor

Valhalla! The archway entrance to the Ferrari factory Maranello, June, 1967. Beyond, Ferrari 330 P4 body panels are being sprayed, the factory working flat out in preparation for Le Mans.

racing was in demand from outside sources wanting a piece of the action and the spin-off publicity.

At the time, most sports were domestic affairs – apart from the Olympic Games – but motor racing was different with Grand Prix events around Europe and beyond. Sponsors were seeking that kind of exposure and, at the Lady Wigram Trophy, New Zealand, January 1968, Jim Clark's Lotus appeared in the colours of John Player's Gold Leaf brand of cigarettes, the car entered by Gold Leaf Team Lotus. Colin Chapman was one of the sport's greatest innovators and new ideas exuded from every pore; extensive advertising had featured on Indycars for years, and Chapman was the first to follow this example in Formula 1.

In this new era the big money came from tobacco companies, reacting to the expected advertising ban on television, but all kinds of unlikely names also came forward: Yardley with BRM; Brooke Bond Oxo with Rob Walker, and even Durex with Surtees' own Formula 1 team! In the early days advertising on Grand Prix cars was crude and unattractive, and entailed a few stickers occupying the limited space permitted at the time. Of course, there was bound to be a backlash. The BBC got very hot under the collar, objecting to cars resembling mobile billboards at 'the centre of the action'. Televised Grand Prix disappeared from BBC screens – not the idea at all as far as the sponsors were concerned! I reacted in my own way by becoming equally hot under the collar, and writing to Sir Charles Curran, Director General of the BBC. The letter reached its target because I received a personal reply from Sir Charles setting out his erudite counter-argument on two foolscap sheets of paper. Only Enzo Ferrari held out against the creeping involvement of unrelated companies, content to give his trade supporters limited exposure on his cars whilst still retaining the overall colour a Ferrari had always been and would remain.

'Wing things'

Early in July 1968 I found myself enjoying hospitality in the faded grandeur of a Normandy chateau, an ornate 19th century brick pile which was home to a Catholic religious order, and just a few minutes' walk across fields to the circuit at Rouen-les-Essarts, venue again for the French Grand Prix that year. Normally, this would have been the 54th Grand Prix de l'Automobile Club de France, the oldest Grand Prix in the world and surely something to be proud of, but there had been a major power struggle and a breakaway organisation calling itself FFSA (Fédération Française du Sport Automobile) had taken over the running of the country's motor sports activities. So it was that the oldest Grand Prix in the calendar suddenly became the 1er Grand Prix de France!

Either way the paddock looked much the same, although practice was now in the late afternoon instead of an uncivilised hour early in the morning, as on my previous visit six years earlier. It is worth remembering that this and other circuits were made up entirely of public roads, and race organisers had to bow to the demands of the local *Gendarmerie* with regard to when they could be closed for practice sessions. The deplorable thing was that the Formula 1 session occupied only fifty minutes on the Thursday and an hour on the Friday, extended by twenty minutes in response to the disgruntled teams who were racing here in 3 litre form for the first time.

The sport had changed utterly since my earlier visit. Outwardly, there were the first indications of sponsorship but, more noticeably, cars were beginning to sprout those weird accretions called 'wings'. I remember standing next to Denny Hulme and hearing his jocular comment to Bruce McLaren: "... wings is in!". How right he was: it was the first real attempt by designers to follow aeronautical principles to ensure that air flow was harnessed and made to work, leading ultimately to the wings, aerofoils, spoilers and barge boards – call them what you will – which have changed the racing car from a thing of beauty to a highly efficient racing machine.

In the past a designer's thinking was to create a 'slippery shape', which inevitably resulted in a thing of beauty. "What looks right is right" was the rule of thumb, and I always found it quite extraordinary that much earlier cars – such as the Maserati 250F and the Vanwall of the fifties – looked absolutely right, as did the 1.5 litre cars of the early sixties. Appearances changed with the 3 litre formula and the 'kit cars' made possible by availability of the Ford-Cosworth V8, once Team Lotus had exhausted its 'exclusive' use at the end of 1967. Some singularly functional-looking cars came about with the engine naked at the rear, and even a layman's mind must have questioned how the air flow coped with the 'hills and troughs' once it passed on behind the driver's head.

Wings began to address that problem, creating tremendous downforce and enabling the wider tyres to be far more effective. Initially, designers were in unknown territory, creating monsters as wings grew in size, not just at the rear but also at the front so that the driver's vision must have been severely impaired. As so often in motor racing, it took a serious accident to encourage radical rethinking of the design implications. Unforeseen loads were being placed on the cars, wings were buckling and suspensions collapsing from the tremendous downforces applied.

At the Spanish Grand Prix in 1969, on the magnificent parkland circuit of Montjuich at Barcelona, the two Team Lotus cars of Graham Hill and Jochen Rindt were involved in separate accidents within a few laps of the start, the direct result of wing failure. Fortunately, no-one was killed that day, but it was a close call and Jochen Rindt ended up in hospital with a hairline fracture of the skull. He was totally opposed to these "wing things", considering them a dangerous irrelevancy.

For the next race at Monaco action was taken following intervention by the CSI. Wings were banned altogether for that event, reappearing for the French Grand Prix at Clermont-Ferrand with strictly limited dimensions, immovable, and no longer fixed to unsprung parts of the car. Those awful front wings disappeared once and for all: common sense had prevailed.

There was a strangely subdued atmosphere in the paddock as practice got under way that Thursday afternoon in 1968 at Rouen-les-Essarts, and the unfolding weekend did nothing to improve that sense of foreboding. Jim Clark had died in a Formula 2 race at Hockenheim three months earlier, Mike Spence (BRM's driver) died in practice at Indianapolis whilst on loan to Lotus, and in June Ludovico Scarfiotti was killed at the Rossfeld hill climb in Germany, driving a Porsche. Motor racing was having to take a close look at itself.

In the fifties the war mentality still prevailed, but by the sixties attitudes were changing and the public was questioning whether this loss of life was appropriate to the new era. If motor racing could not get its house in order, perhaps others should do it? Of course, nothing is that easy. Grand Prix racing has always pushed the boundaries – that is the fundamental ethos of its existence. As always, self-regulation was the only way, which is how it has continued to this day.

1968 witnessed the emergence of an important new team: Matra International, brainchild of Ken Tyrrell, who was already known as a successful entrant in Formula 2 with French Matra cars. His new venture came about because of the availability of the Ford-Cosworth V8 DFV (as it was known – Double Four Valve), and he used a Matra chassis in direct competition with Matra's own V12 engined cars. Jackie Stewart was emerging as the natural successor to Jim Clark, something Ken Tyrrell recognised when enticing him away from BRM, where Jackie was doubtless concerned at BRM's apparent loss of confidence in the H16 engine, and transfer in 1968 to the V12, originally intended as an engine for sale. It was a brave move for Stewart, and the right one, as a remarkable relationship developed between the two men which resulted in World Championship titles for Stewart in 1969, 1971 and 1973, and the Constructor's title for Tyrrell's own chassis in 1971. The two rival Matra teams were already a considerable force by the time they arrived at Rouen-les Essarts, having finished first (Stewart) and second (Jean-Pierre Beltoise) in the Dutch Grand Prix at Zandvoort two weeks earlier.

Jochen Rindt was like a boy with a new skateboard at Rouen, his Brabham BT26 Repco V8 absolutely right for him for the first time that season, having moved on from Cooper at the end of 1967. He was the lap record holder here already and clearly the circuit suited his style, as he put in the fastest lap during Thursday's opening practice which nobody came within a second of matching on either day. Sadly, Jochen Rindt will always be remembered as Formula 1's first and only posthumous World Champion, as he died at the wheel of a Lotus 72C during practice for the Italian Grand Prix at Monza in 1970, having already secured sufficient points for the title.

The adrenalin must have been rushing for Jackie Oliver too, but for all the wrong reasons because he became the first to experience the effects of wing failure at high speed. Expert opinion suggests that the fabricated bracket of a supporting pillar for the wing failed in the extremes of air turbulence following another car along Rouen's finishing straight. The wing folded back at 190mph (306kph), lifting the rear wheels clear of the road, instantly sending the Lotus out of control. The car hit a brick pillar on which was mounted the high wrought iron gates of a disused drive to the chateau where I was staying. The wing, gearbox and entire rear suspension were torn off before the remainder of the car, including the 'driver', finally came to a halt. The strength of the monocoque saved Oliver's life, and he walked away with nothing more than minor cuts and bruises.

Just as I remember Jochen Rindt full of ebullience as he talked to boss Jack Brabham about the performance of his car that day, so an ashen-faced Jackie Oliver explained the circumstances of his dreadful accident to a concerned Colin Chapman. Oliver had been drafted into the Lotus team to take the place of Jim Clark, an invidious position for a driver new to this top level of motor racing. The Lotus 49Bs arrived at Rouen with massive rear wings standing on tall struts mounted, unusually, on the suspension uprights, whereas other cars had wings mounted on the chassis. It was a typically daring approach by Colin Chapman but it put stresses on components which they were not designed to take. Notwithstanding that, Graham Hill raced next day in the remaining 49B!

Bruce McLaren took advantage of the availability of the Ford-Cosworth V8 in 1968 to resolve the engine supply problems for his enthusiastic team, and World Champion Denny Hulme joined him to form an all-Kiwi partnership. Between them they had already won two important non-championship races earlier in the season: the Race of Champions at Brands Hatch and the traditional *Daily Express* International Trophy at Silverstone, the latter a resounding first and second for these always immaculate, orangey-yellow type M7As. It sounds a dreadful colour scheme but, in fact, it looked superb!

It is interesting to reflect that national newspapers were an important part of motor racing in those days, particularly the *Daily Express*, which supported the very first International Trophy Race in 1949. The newspaper became synonymous with Silverstone for many years, also supporting the Grand Prix and giving the races huge advance publicity; I have scrapbooks full of contemporary cuttings. Maybe in an effort to emulate its rival, the *Daily Mail* stepped in with support for a Formula 1 race at Brands Hatch, later to become the Race of Champions, which was a new event for 1965 and continued for years. Other events included the *Daily Telegraph* Aintree 200, and the Tourist Trophy at Goodwood in the late fifties extrovertly supported by the *News of the World*. Sponsorship, by any other name, has always been around ...

Incredibly, the Grand Prix at Rouen did not start until after 4 o'clock in the afternoon, following supporting races that went on all day and an interminable lunch interval. The weather had been ominous throughout and a heavy shower of rain was falling as the Grand Prix cars were lining up for the start. Jacky Ickx was the only driver to opt for full 'wet' tyres, decided by the toss of a

Just beyond the start and finish plateau was a perfect belvedere from which to watch the race. This is a preliminary national saloon car race with a wrecked Renault on the right as an ambulance leaves the circuit on the left. The race continues unabated! Note the complete absence of Armco. French Grand Prix, Rouen-les-Essarts, 1968.

coin with his Ferrari team-mate Chris Amon, who started on 'dry' weather tyres. As a consequence, Ickx quickly grabbed the lead from Stewart's Matra halfway round the first lap and just drove away from everybody in an amazingly mature performance for a driver in his first full year of Formula 1. Jacky Ickx was inspirational to watch in any car and wet conditions were his *forte*. It was in Sports and Prototypes that his exploits are best remembered: winning at Le Mans a total of six times in Ferraris and Porsches, and his most famous victory in the Ford GT40 in 1969 when he won the race by a few metres.

It was on the third lap of the Grand Prix that disaster struck. Standing on the belvedere high above the circuit beyond the start and finish point, where I had watched the race in 1962, we were suddenly aware of a thick column of black smoke rising above the trees down toward the Nouveau-Monde Hairpin. It was a sight which was not unknown in those days, witnessed with the utmost apprehension. Anthony Marsh was giving an English commentary, as he did at many of the continental circuits as well as at Silverstone, and I anxiously waited for information about what was surely a serious accident. It transpired that veteran French driver Jo Schlesser had lost control of his Honda V8 on the last streaming wet right-hander before the hairpin. The car ran wide and slid up the sloping grass bank toward a spectator enclosure, overturned and caught fire, instantly becoming a raging inferno due to nearly full fuel tanks. The driver had no chance of survival,

and burning petrol and magnesium showered spectators, a fiery barrier spreading across the road. Somehow, following drivers managed to squeeze through. There was no question of the race being stopped, and pace cars were unknown. The show must go on was the guiding principle.

The story behind the tragedy was wrapped in controversy. Honda had grabbed John Surtees for its 1967 campaign. John was keen to move on from Cooper even though he had won the last race of 1966 with the Maserati V12 engined car – the Mexican Grand Prix. For 1967 the whole Honda programme revolved around John Surtees, known for his Ferrari years, his World Championship in 1964, and his ability to master a car and get results. He won one race in 1967 at Monza after an exciting battle with Jack Brabham in what was an otherwise barren year. For 1968 Honda concentrated on developing the engines, leaving Surtees to continue developing the chassis in conjunction with Eric Broadley of Lola at Slough, the car irreverently referred to as the 'Hondola' and already winner at Monza the previous year. The intrinsic problem lay with the underpowered V12 engine, and eventually Honda started afresh, producing an air-cooled V8 in a new chassis (type RA302) designed and built in Japan and brought to England for Surtees to test. Surtees made it very clear that the new car needed further development and that he would be concentrating on his water-cooled V12 (type RA301) for the French race.

Mr Soichiro Honda was in Paris and wanted the new car raced to promote Honda's presence in the French marketplace. It was also considered important to have a French driver in the cockpit and, to add to the French connection, the car was entered by Honda France. Jo Schlesser was forty years old at the time, but inexperienced in Formula 1 and out of his depth with this difficult handling car which had had minimal advance testing. The tragic consequence of the accident was another slur on the declining reputation of Formula 1 at that time and John Surtees' despondent expression in the paddock afterwards said it all. Grand Prix drivers seemed to be carved from granite and, despite repeatedly passing the scene of the terrible accident which had befallen his team-mate, John Surtees nevertheless succeeded in finishing second in what was Honda's best result that year.

A V8 engined car turned up at Monza for David Hobbs to

try in pre-practice for the Italian Grand Prix in September, but then effectively the project was abandoned. Honda withdrew from racing at the end of the season and John Surtees went off to drive for BRM in 1969, a glutton for punishment.

Jackie Stewart had another good finish at Rouen in third place for Matra International, and fourth was Vic Elford in the works-entered Cooper T86B, Cooper now using BRM's V12 engine instead of the weighty Maserati V12. (Elford had enjoyed a glittering rallying career long before he turned to racing, chiefly in Sports and Prototype cars.) Denny Hulme was fifth and Piers Courage sixth in a BRM V12, the latter a driver who has come to the fore in recent years with the publication of a book about his life and death at Zandvoort in 1970. After such promising form in practice Jochen Rindt failed to finish and Jean-Pierre Beltoise in the Matra V12, entered by the factory Matra-Sports, was ninth, four laps in arrears.

Prior to late afternoon practice on the Friday I had been looking around a pretty village a bus ride away beside the River Seine, only to find the Matra-Sports team tucked away in a garage. All day the car was being feverishly worked upon, with a few locals and I standing around watching a new V12 engine being installed, and hoping the mechanics would eventually fire it up. As the afternoon wore on and the time for practice approached, a car drew up outside and Jean-Pierre stepped out already in his racing overalls. Our patience was rewarded at last as a mechanic squirted petrol from the nozzle of a plastic bottle into the injection trumpets, which was followed by a laborious metallic note as the starter motor struggled to turn over the engine from a slave battery. After a few hesitant, abortive attempts it spluttered reluctantly into life, firstly on a few cylinders until eventually it was running cleanly. The mechanic pulled on the throttle cable to build up the revs, at the same time getting the oil and water up to temperature before, finally, a series of short, sharp stabs of ear-shattering sound left us onlookers dazed. We were deaf, our eyes were streaming, and we were choking on carbon monoxide fumes, but it was sheer Heaven, an experience that any enthusiast of the time will recognise! Jean-Pierre put on a fire mask and helmet, donned driving gloves and eased himself into the tight cockpit, revving the engine and moving somewhat hesitantly on the clutch out into the road. There was a blast of sound as he cleared the car's coughs and protests, and then he simply drove off down the main street behind a Citroën support car and up into the hills to the circuit for final practice. Not a *Gendarme* to be seen!

To conclude ...

Following Jim Clark's death at Hockenheim early in 1968, it would have been reasonable to expect that Lotus's fortunes would collapse, so strong had been the bond between him and Colin Chapman. However, such was the fortitude of Graham Hill that he quickly raised the team from its knees and brought it new success, ultimately claiming the World Championship for both Driver and Constructor at the end of that fateful season.

Graham was a colossus of his time, and nobody should be misled by the oft voiced opinion that he lacked Clark's natural talent. That may be so, but he applied himself rigorously to his craft and combined it with extraordinary courage and versatility, which enabled him to get the best from his cars, his mechanics and those close to him. He was World Champion twice, won at Le Mans and also the Indianapolis 500 – a record of achievements which can never be matched. Moreover he was a wonderful ambassador for his sport, supported by an adoring public, but with another side to his character, less recognised in his public persona. As a perfectionist he was incredibly demanding of other people, a trait that often made him difficult to work with. It was Graham Hill who brought supreme success to BRM and later took Team Lotus to new heights from its lowest point earlier in the year.

"... revving the engine and moving somewhat hesitantly on the clutch out into the road". Jean-Pierre Beltoise leaves the team's garage in a nearby village after an engine change and drives his Matra V12 type MS11 to the circuit for final practice. He qualified on the third row but finished 9th – all but Ickx being on the wrong tyres. French Grand Prix, Rouen-les-Essarts, 1968.

14th May 1960
Daily Express International Trophy
SILVERSTONE

Graham Hill looks on as his BRM P48 (chassis 482) is unloaded from an Austin Lodestar which BRM had used since the V16 days. It was the last event for three such vehicles, plus the large mobile petrol driven Commer workshop in the background. Thereafter BRM used a new diesel engined Leyland Tiger with purpose-built body by Marshalls of Cambridge. The team's new transport arrangements saved hugely on transportation costs. This was BRM's first rear-engined car. Note the fireproof rubberised fuel tanks, replacing the old welded aluminium tanks which were prone to split on impact.

Stirling Moss chatting with Tommy Sopwith, left (patron of Equipe Endeavour Ltd.), and team-mate Jack Sears in the pits during practice.

Stirling Moss and the Jaguar 3.8 MkII in which he finished 2nd to Roy Salvadori's similar car in the Production Touring Car Race.

1959 World Champion Jack Brabham's latest 'low-line' Cooper Climax 4 cylinder type 53. Jack went on to win his second World Championship with this car in 1960.

Phil Hill's Ferrari D246 V6. He and team-mate Cliff Allison finished 5th and 8th. These front engined cars were by now overwhelmed by the British rear engined revolution. Roll on 1961 ... !

Phil Hill's car as in the previous photo.

Team manager Romulo Tavoni watches as chief mechanic Adelmo Marchetti fuels Allison's Ferrari.

The Border Reivers Aston Martin DBR1/300 with helmeted Jim Clark ready for practice. Jim and Roy Salvadori finished third at Le Mans with this car a few weeks later. The tail had been modified to comply with 'luggage' capacity dimensions for Le Mans 1958.

Scuderia Centro-Sud *ran Cooper Maseratis, but without success.*

Ex-motorcycle World Champion Geoff Duke tried four wheels but without much success. Here he is in a Gemini Formula Junior car entered by Graham Warner's company The Chequered Flag Ltd.

The Aston Martin DBR4/250s of No 7 Maurice Trintignant and No 6 Roy Salvadori. These front-engined cars were outdated even before they entered Formula 1 at this same event the previous year. Sadly, they were out of Formula 1 before mid-season 1960.

Stirling Moss getting ready to leave the circuit in his Triumph Herald.

Mike Salmon in his Jaguar D Type. These famous cars were beginning to have a vintage look about them, their achievements at Le Mans a part of history!

'End of the day'. Ferrari's Adelmo Marchetti rests wearily against Cliff Allison's D246 prior to loading for return to Heathrow.

6th May 1961 — Daily Express International Trophy SILVERSTONE

Dan Gurney talks to Mrs Louise Bryden-Brown, American entrant of his Lotus 18 in the 'Intercontinental' race for the redundant 2.5 litre Formula 1 cars. (Formula 1 from 1961 was for 1.5 litre cars.) Dan was a non-starter. He was the first driver to use the 'over the ears' Bell Star helmet. In Formula 1 Dan, together with Jo Bonnier, drove for Porsche but they were frustrated awaiting the new type 804 which did not appear until 1962.

14th Apr 1962 — International Lombank Trophy Meeting
SNETTERTON

Behind the Surtees Lola can be seen the ex-works 4 cylinder Porsche of Wolfgang Seidel.

Rhodesian Tony Maggs with the Ken Tyrrell-entered Cooper FIII.

John Surtees and team manager Reg Parnell discuss the Formula 1 Lola Climax 4 cylinder, awaiting delivery of their first Coventry-Climax V8 engine. The Bowmaker Yeoman Racing Team was created around John Surtees with Roy Salvadori as his team-mate. Surtees retired from this race due to overheating problems. The Bowmaker Yeoman name disappeared when John Surtees joined Ferrari for 1963, though the Lolas continued to be raced under the Reg Parnell banner.

12th May 1962 — *Daily Express* **International Trophy SILVERSTONE**

Mechanic Pat Carvath ready to tow-start Graham Hill's BRM V8 type P578. This once troubled team was now rejuvenated – they sensed they had a winning car and they were right! Note the old concrete runway breaking up.

The 'chimney stack' exhausts gave the new BRMs a very purposeful appearance, but were discontinued and replaced with low level exhausts by the Belgian Grand Prix in June. This is Richie Ginther's car with mechanic Arthur Hill fastening the bodywork. Graham Hill started from pole and won the race, but Richie crashed badly and wrote-off this car.

The BRM fuel injected V8 engine, and the large aluminium oil tank for the 5 speed gearbox secured above it by 'spider' cords.

Porsche 4 cylinder ex-Formula 2 car of Scuderia SSS Republica di Venezia driven by Jo Bonnier. In red livery it looked good.

Bruce McLaren (in cockpit bleeding the brakes) chose to drive Tommy Atkins' earlier 4 cylinder Climax-engined Cooper as the Cooper team was still awaiting an adequate supply of Coventry Climax V8 engines. He finished 5th.

Car No 9 is the Ferrari V6 type 156 with the latest 120 degree engine driven by Innes Ireland. The car was on loan to the UDT-Laystall team as a goodwill gesture by Enzo Ferrari following Stirling Moss' accident at Goodwood a few weeks earlier, in the Lotus 18/21 Climax V8 which the team had borrowed from Rob Walker. Also in the picture is the Lotus 19 with a 2.7 Climax engine driven to victory by Ireland in the sports car race. Finally, Masten Gregory, Mauro Forghieri and Franco Gozzi, Ferrari's Press Officer on the left, pore over the Lotus 24 Climax V8 which Gregory drove into 8th place in the Trophy race.

The 1962 Ferrari type 156 was looked after by factory mechanics, and a pale green stripe was painted down the middle in deference to the UDT-Laystall team's colour. Mauro Forghieri (here doing his calculations) was lately out of Bologna University and worked for Ferrari, just as did his father before him on the Alfa Romeo 158s run by Scuderia Ferrari in the thirties. Innes Ireland finished 4th but disliked the handling of the car, though the engine "... revved like hell."! Plans had been well advanced for Rob Walker to be loaned a factory Ferrari F1 car for Stirling to drive in 1962, even painted in the dark blue of RRC Walker Racing Team. Sadly, a case of what might have been ...

This beautiful Ferrari GTO had just been delivered to UDT-Laystall and painted in the team's apple green livery. Masten Gregory put it to good use immediately, finishing 2nd to Mike Parkes' similar car in the GT race for the Scalextric Trophy!

Jim Clark talking to Lotus mechanics Dick Scammel (partially hidden) and chief mechanic Jim Endruweit. Clark, who was driving a Lotus 24 Climax V8 in the Trophy event, was beaten into 2nd place on the line by Graham Hill in a thrilling broadside finish in torrential rain.

Cyril Atkins, ex-Vanwall chief mechanic and now chief mechanic at BRM, checks Richie Ginther's type P578 prior to practice, watched by Arthur Hill. Despite their problems of a decade or more, BRMs were always superbly finished and here they looked more beautiful than ever in the familiar dark green team colour.

1st July 1962 — Grand Prix (non-championship) DE REIMS

"... no wider than the average 'B' road today ...". The N31 – the Soissons Straight – with the Thillois Hairpin in the hazy distance, prior to road closure for evening practice.

Exit from Thillois Hairpin. Moss used to go up the escape road past the café-bar (on the left) on leaving the Soissons Straight, thus entering the final straight and crossing the start line at higher speed to begin a fast practice lap, hopefully achieving a better grid position.

Rhodesian Tony Maggs (centre), Cooper's No 2 driver, talks to English commentator Anthony Marsh (holding clipboard) whilst Bruce McLaren, in spotless overalls (right), seems suspicious of the man behind the lens. Bruce won the race in a 1962 Cooper-Climax V8, whilst Maggs had to use the older Tommy Atkins Cooper-Climax 4 cylinder which Bruce had used at Silverstone (see page 81). Maggs retired after twenty two laps.

Bruce McLaren's 1962 Cooper-Climax V8, the second to be built. The engine's exhausts were quite different from those of the Lotus 25 Climax V8.

Innes Ireland, one arm round Jean Ginther, exchanges a joke with team-mate Masten Gregory, who seems more concerned with lighting his pipe! Both drove Lotus 24s for UDT-Laystall. Ireland finished 3rd with a Climax V8 but Gregory retired the BRM V8-engined car. Ireland's career was in decline; Colin Chapman fired him at the end of 1961 despite his having just achieved the first Championship victory for Team Lotus – the U.S. GP at Watkins Glen. Chapman chose to invest in Jim Clark for the long-term future of his team and Ireland never forgave him.

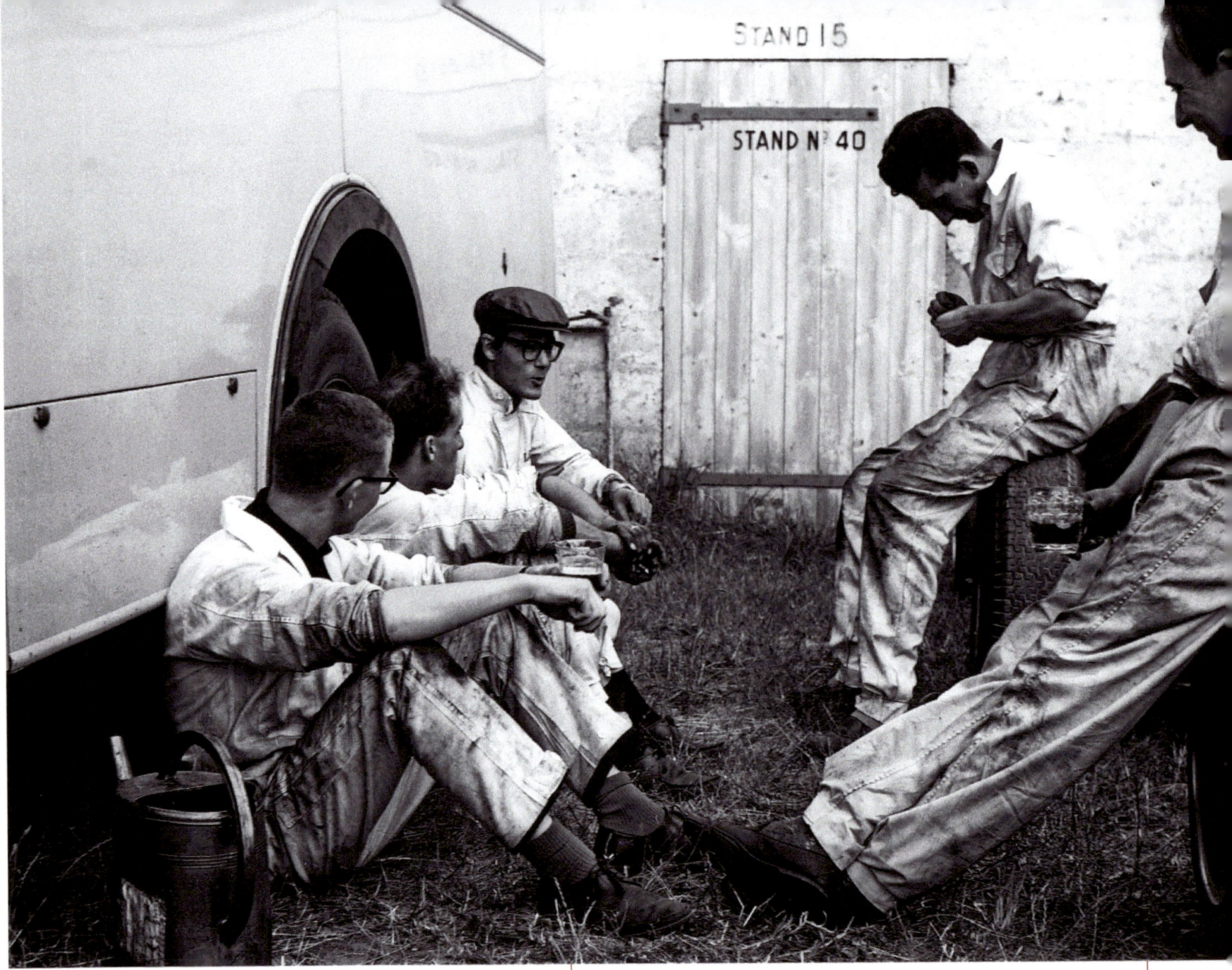

Masten Gregory (wearing pebble lens glasses) chats with his weary mechanics enjoying a warm beer. Masten was always a great favourite with the crowds but died in Italy at the age of 53 from a heart attack.

American Masten Gregory enthuses about the Chrysler V8 engine in Rob Walker's Facel Vega (Rob is in the centre). A mechanic takes a break from racing cars to look at the front suspension.

A suave Roy Salvadori and incredibly youthful John Surtees. Both drove Lola Climax V8s for Bowmaker-Yeoman. It is difficult to appreciate that Surtees was already a multi-World Champion on two wheels!

The two Lola drivers talking to Dunlop's Vic Barlow. Not all enthusiasts of the day wore a Homburg hat!

Carel Godin de Beaufort unloading his 4 cylinder Porsche. He came from a titled Dutch family, a respected and well-liked amateur who drove his elderly Porsche with great skill and consistency amidst much more sophisticated machinery. Sadly, he died aged just 30 after an accident at the Nürburgring whilst practising for the German Grand Prix of 1964. Here he finished 7th, inches ahead of Jo Bonnier's similar car.

Officials of the organising club wore straw hats with coloured identification ribbons. Here, the BRM's front suspension is the subject of their attention, whilst a pipe-smoking Raymond Mays reassures them! The V8 receives a set of 'hard' plugs.

Trevor Taylor (left) explaining to BRM's Tony Rudd (in glasses) that the 'customer' V8 in his Lotus 24 has failed to produce the expected power. Note that this 'customer' engine still used the early 'chimney stack' exhausts, whereas BRM's own cars had low-level exhausts by this time. For the race Taylor drove a '24' with Climax V8 engine, but crashed lightly at Thillois on the 2nd lap when petrol from a front fuel tank leaked onto the pedals.

A contemplative Raymond Mays (right) looks on as Pat Carvath readies Graham Hill's BRM V8 P578. Graham discusses the car with chief engineer Tony Rudd, in shirtsleeves. Graham came second in the race but Richie retired.

Old team-mates Bruce McLaren and Jack Brabham, now rivals, chat with Cooper mechanic Mike Grohman. No immaculate sponsor's overalls, just a pencil behind the ear! Brabham (centre) finished the race fourth.

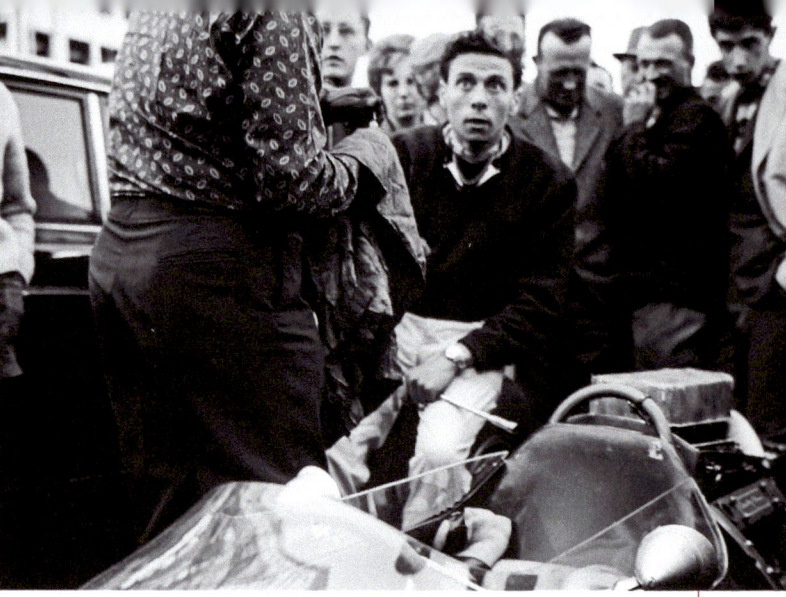

Jim Clark, not averse to getting his hands dirty, changes the plugs of his Climax V8.

Jack Brabham in his Lotus 24 Climax V8, sans bodywork. Leaving Cooper and setting up his own team for 1962 had not been without its problems. A fire at his factory seriously damaged his Lotus early in the season, and he was unable to debut his Brabham car until the German Grand Prix in August.

Rob Walker and French journalist Gerard 'Jabby' Crombac (left) share an amusing moment with a race official. 'Jabby' was the doyen of motoring journalists and died in 2006, writing about cars until the end.

Cars lining up at the pits for practice. The two works Coopers are there: the white car with a blue stripe is a Cooper Special driven by Ian Burgess which finished 11th in the race, 5 laps in arrears! Bruce McLaren and Tony Maggs can be seen walking past the back of the car.

Service support vehicles in a Reims side street, Dunlop's tyre fitters preparing for evening practice.

BRM's magnificent Leyland Tiger transporter (described on page 70) in which the author hitched a lift back into town after practice.

8th July 1962 — French Grand Prix ROUEN-LES-ESSARTS

Alf Francis (right) and Tony Cleverly fuel the dark blue liveried Lotus 24 Climax V8 of Rob Walker's team. Driven by Frenchman Maurice Trintignant, the car was written off in a disastrous incident at the end of the race.

Swedish driver Jo Bonnier, "... a seldom smiling and serious man ..." (centre) with chief mechanic Alf Francis (right), and team owner Rob Walker just in the picture on the left. Jo was to drive Walker's cars in the future, once his involvement with Porsche ended after 1962. He was a late retirement here with the second of the new flat 8-cylinder Porsches.

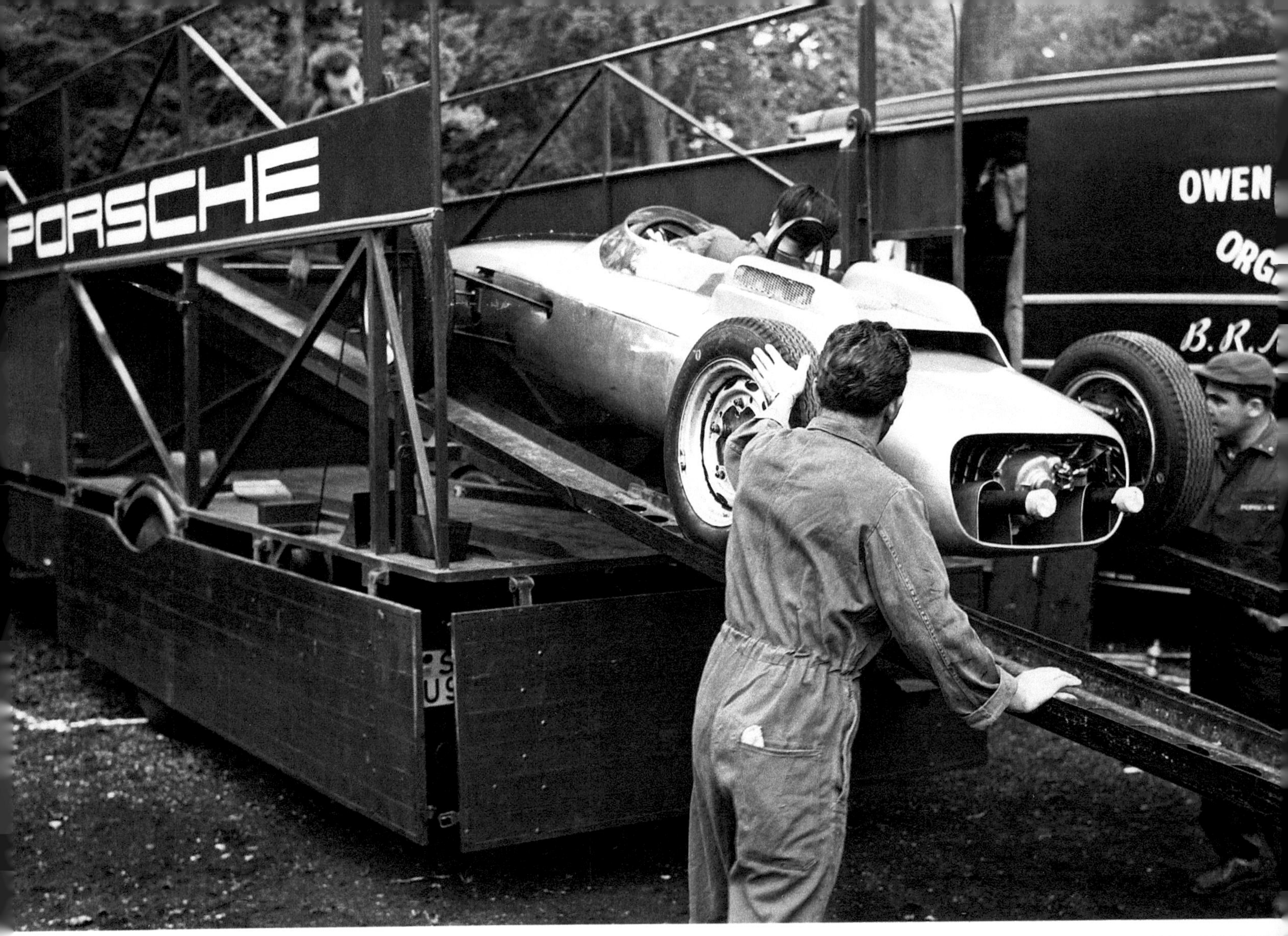
PORSCHE
OWEN

YEOMAN RACING

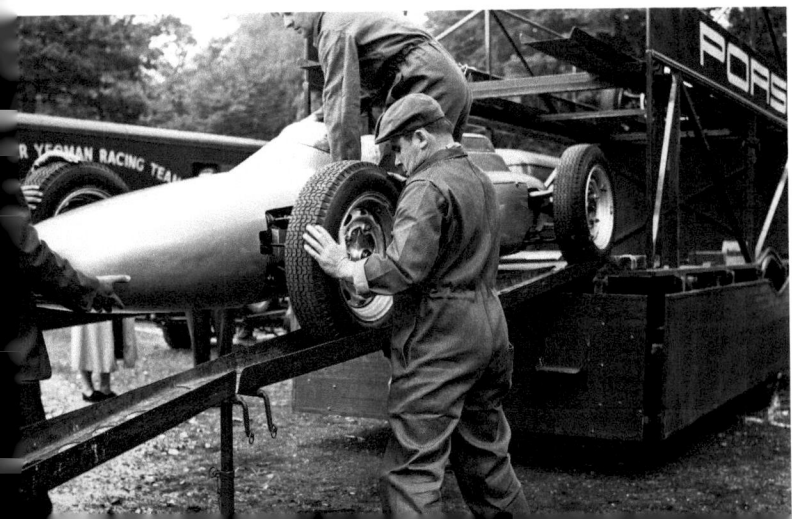

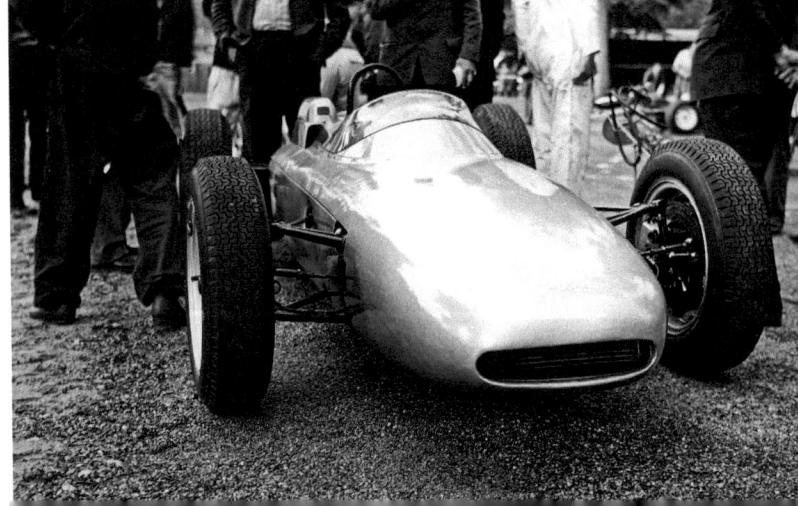

The Porsche team brought its exciting cars to Rouen after extensive testing at the Nürburgring, following a disappointing start to the season. Note the large plastic cooling fan above the flat 8 air cooled engine. The gearbox had 6 speeds. The type 804s tubular chassis already looked dated alongside Colin Chapman's innovative monocoque Lotus 25, "body panels simply covering the mechanical bits".

Tall Dan Gurney had a job to fit into the tight Porsche cockpit! He inherited the lead after Clark and Graham Hill retired and went on to win the Grand Prix in 2 hours, 7 minutes, 35 seconds – 164kph.

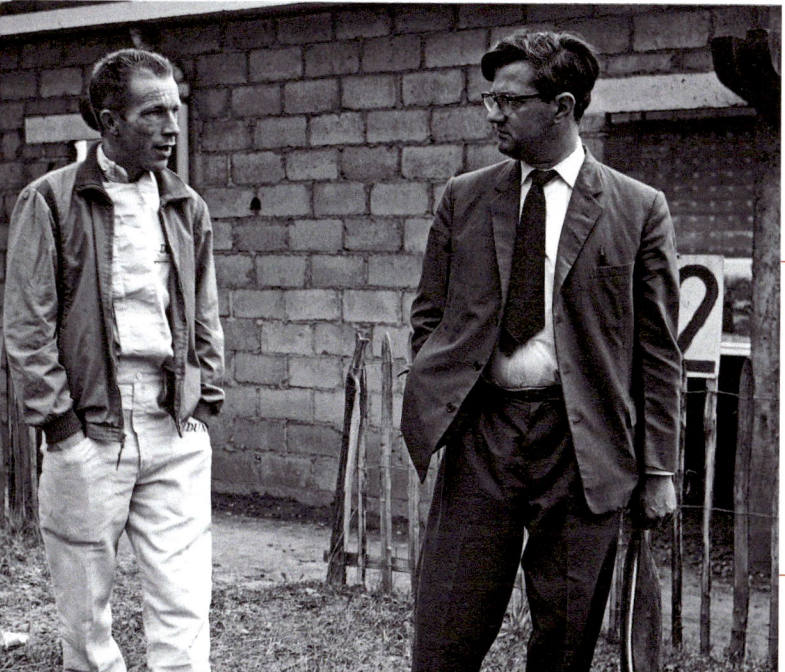

One of the author's favourite photographs is Louis Klementaski's shot of a Lancia-Ferrari amongst the trees of the paddock at Rouen in the early morning sunshine, 1957. My own imitated offering is of Pat Carvath attaching a tow rope to Graham Hill's BRM, and Arthur Hill about to get into the tow car.

Diminutive Richie Ginther, BRM's No 2 driver, here talking to chief engineer Tony Rudd, who was to leave for Lotus in September 1969 after experiencing the highs and lows of BRM for 19 years. The ever-resourceful Ginther had the throttle cable snap at the pedal with 5 laps remaining, but stopped out on the circuit and wound the cable round his hand, displaying a clenched fist every time he passed the pits! He finished the race in 3rd place.

6th Aug 1962 — International Guards Trophy
BRANDS HATCH

All ready for the start of practice in the early morning sunshine. Colin Chapman and Jim Clark are clearly visible, 'Jenks' as ever is beavering information and Porsche team manager, von Hanstein, looks on as Dan Gurney settles into his car. Note the faded slogan painted on the track "Vive de Gaulle" and the Croix de Lorraine, French Grand Prix, Rouen-les-Essarts, 1962.

The fearsome 'beautifully ugly' 4 litre V8 Maserati 151 entered by Maserati France. The Maserati had been tested on the autostrada at 186mph. Belgian Lucien Bianchi was to drive the car, but it broke an oil line whilst being warmed up in the paddock and failed to take the start. Only three of these cars were built and this one appears again on page 138 with a 4.9 litre engine and different colour scheme. Re-bodied in 1964, it was destroyed during the April Le Mans trials of 1965 and its driver, Lloyd Casner, was killed.

Jo Bonnier (in cockpit) finished 3rd in the main event for Sports and Prototype cars with this 3 litre V12 Ferrari Testa Rossa entered by Scuderia SSS Republica di Venezia. The car was off-loaded from the Scuderia Serenissima transporter (right), historically somewhat confusing! The cars of private teams were worked hard and often looked quite tatty.

Jaguar racing saloons always attracted the best drivers with highly professional teams such as John Coombs car No107 seen here and Equipe Endeavour *entering two cars apiece. Here, Graham Hill could be signing anything, wholly focused as he is on his work.*

Dick Protheroe was always a competitive privateer, and his lightweight Jaguar E Type always immaculately turned out.

High profile entrant John Coombs with his two drivers Graham Hill and the urbane Roy Salvadori. Both were driving his Jaguar 3.8 MkIIs. Graham hit the bank and 'Salvo' lost his exhaust in the Molyslip Trophy for Saloon Cars but finished 3rd. The pair also drove a Coombs E Type and a new GTO respectively in the GT race for the Peco Trophy.

Carlo Abate drove a specially-bodied 250 GT Ferrari, popularly known as the 'bread van' because of its van-like appearance at the rear. It was entered by Scuderia SSS Republica di Venezia, and finished 4th in the Sports and Prototypes event.

The Ferrari being fuelled for practice.

"... like a leopard on wheels ...". The glorious Ferrari GTO of Maranello Concessionaires driven by John Surtees. He spun at South Bank bend in the dreadful conditions and eventually finished 4th in the GT race. In these photos John Coombs in the white shirt seems to be enthusing with Col Ronnie Hoare (Chairman of Maranello Concessionaires) about his recently delivered GTO. 36 GTOs were built, all of which still exist today, including this one (chassis 3647GT). This particular car is unusual in that after delivery Maranello Concessionaires added a third air vent and twin rows of louvres to the bonnet. South Bank can be seen in the background.

The spartan interior of John Surtees' Ferrari. The complete absence of any form of roll-cage is very noticeable. Note the enormous gear lever and open-gate gear change. Also the 'agricultural' looking handbrake.

Mike Parkes hand blips the Ferrari's throttle mechanism and produces that unmistakeable V12 roar! Note the crackle finish of the cam covers and those six handsome air-gulping double-choke Weber carburettors.

6th Oct 1962 — *The Motor* International Six Hours Saloon Car Race **Brands Hatch**

The Equipe Endeavour *Jaguar 3.8. MkII shared by Bruce Halford and Roy Pierpoint. It was one of seven cars that lost wheels in this endurance event but pitted and continued, eventually back in the pits again for a lengthy stay before emerging for a final lap in overdrive top to claim the team prize for Jaguar.*

Tommy Sopwith, son of aviation pioneer Sir Thomas Sopwith and Patron of Equipe Endeavour, *lends a hand, here siphoning air from the petrol tank to ensure maximum capacity during fuelling.*

Bruce Halford, in the second Endeavour Jaguar, *deputised for injured Norfolk farmer Jack Sears (right), spectating here, following a bad crash in the Tour de France Automobile, and only just released from a French hospital. Here, Jack discusses Jaguar handling with Jimmy Blumer, who co-drove the winning* Endeavour Jaguar *with Mike Parkes.*

There were five 'capacity' classes, and third overall was a tiny Mini Cooper driven by Cooper expert John Aley and a certain Denny Hulme, finishing behind two Jaguars. The two 'works' Mini Coopers were always immaculate in BRG with two white stripes down the bonnet and a white roof. The team even ran to a 'T' (training) car! The pastoral scene in the background disappeared long ago, taken over by the extended paddock and the M20 motorway.

Dunlop was the dominant tyre manufacturer in every major category in the early sixties.

Trade support was low-key; "Their participation ... discreet, in fact, barely recognised ...".

Everybody lent a hand, and here Mike Parkes assists with paddock preparation "... invariably wearing a tweed jacket and suede shoes ...".

11th May 1963
Daily Express International Trophy
SILVERSTONE

It was early morning and chilly, but there was really no excuse for 'Big John's' hat! Two of these latest Ferrari type 156s, with proven 120 degree V6 engines but still with tubular space frames, were sent to Silverstone for John Surtees and Willy Mairesse to drive. Undoubtedly John's experience with British cars in 1962 influenced the new design, particularly the rear suspension. At last Ferrari was using own designed and manufactured 'knock-off' cast alloy wheels, forsaking wire spoked wheels.

"The cars looked good and those high revving engines sounded superb!". Chief mechanic Cyril Atkins manoeuvres Richie Ginther's BRM V8 P578 as engine man Willie Southcott (in Pac-a-Mac) looks on. Both Richie's and Graham Hill's BRMs retired from the race.

John Surtees' 'typical' Ferrari cockpit and, as ever, a beautifully-shaped car. The driving position was reclined, with the 6 speed gearbox lever on the driver's left.

Pat Carvath unloads Graham Hill's BRM, watched closely by Carel Godin de Beaufort (left). Graham used this actual car ('lightweight' type P578 No.5785) to win the 1962 World Championship in South Africa. The hoped for monocoque did not appear until mid-1963, delayed by priority work on the Rover-BRM project (see page 122).

Arthur Hill gently guides BRM V8 type 578 down the ramp, to be officially handed over to 'Mimmo' Dei's Scuderia Centro-Sud. This was chassis No 5781, the first of the type 578s, debuted at the initial Formula 1 race of 1962 in Brussels. Here, the car was painted red and driven by Lorenzo Bandini, but disqualified from the race for receiving a push-start after a pit stop. This car, in its original 'chimney stack' form, can be seen in the photograph on page 79.

"... they could be inhospitable places, even on a summer's day!". That seems to be how Willy Mairesse feels about Silverstone. He crashed the new Ferrari at Stowe early in the race. Mairesse had a reputation as being something of a crasher, often referred to as 'Wild Willy'. Sadly, he took his own life in 1969 once his motor racing career ground to a halt after numerous injuries.

Above & left: The latest 1963 Cooper-Climax V8 type T66. The cars were driven by Bruce McLaren and Tony Maggs, finishing 2nd and 6th respectively. Tony Maggs' No 7 was so new it had not been painted; the bodywork can be seen leaning against the fence! Note the technical artist, clipboard in hand. Cooper used its own design 6-speed gearbox. The substantial, straight forward tubular space frame was clothed in attractive aluminium bodywork, presented in Cooper's dark green colour scheme (almost black), with two white stripes down the front to distinguish them from the privately owned cars.

The works Lotus Climax V8 type 25 with and without exhaust tail pipes "... like the barrels of a gun aimed at the opposition behind." The Lotuses were beautifully finished, as can be seen from the chromed drive shafts. Note the inboard 'doughnut' universal coupling.

Rob Walker's French Chrysler engined Facel Vega proudly displaying his BRDC badge.

Willy Mairesse and Mauro Forghieri.

Jim Clark, always smiling, ready for the start of practice. He was 6th on the grid but won the race in his Lotus 25 Climax V8. At the end of the day's practice there was an untimed half-hour 'free-for-all' session, Formula 1 cars mixing it with Minis and Formula Juniors.

John Surtees' Ferrari with mechanic in familiar "... beret and brown overalls".

John Surtees all ready to go, with Team Manager Eugenio Dragoni looking on (right). Surtees retired with no engine oil left, having trailed smoke for most of the race!

The familiar Ferrari 120 degree V6 in the Surtees car. Surtees did not consider the V6 a match for the Climax and BRM V8s. It had the power but would not run reliably above 10,000rpm. Ferrari was experimenting with alternative V8 and Flat 12 designs at this time, much of which was a distraction as far as Surtees was concerned.

15-16 June 1963 *Vingt Quatre Heures* **LE MANS**

Les Hunaudières *bar/restaurant* on the Mulsanne Straight where it was possible to sit on the terrace and watch cars passing at nearly 200mph on the other side of the straw bales!

Out of Terte Rouge on to the so-called Mulsanne 'Straight', the road open for normal use prior to practice. Those straw bales seem to be the wrong side of the tree!

The Rover-BRM gas turbine car driven by BRM team drivers Graham Hill and Richie Ginther. The car was competing in a demonstration run for a special prize, hence No '00'. It exceeded all targets, completing 4173km at an average speed of 174kph. It would have finished 7th in overall classification. BRM's John Sismey eases the car down the ramps.

The Lola GT with the Ford Cortina MkI rear lights! This new car was far from ready for its first race and missed scrutineering, risking exclusion. Fortunately, co-operation all round got it into the race driven by David Hobbs and Richard Attwood, where it performed well until the gearbox played up and Hobbs hit both banks at the Esses trying to select 3rd gear early on Sunday morning. Here, Eric Broadley (facing) discusses rear view visibility with an official. The car used a 4.7 litre American Ford V8 engine. This car was the forerunner of the much more famous Ford GT 40.

Scuderia Ferrari *unloading a precious cargo of 3 litre V12 prototypes, the 250 Ps. No 21, the winning car, was driven by Lorenzo Bandini and Ludovico Scarfiotti. No 22 with Mike Parkes and Umberto Maglioli finished 3rd, and No 23 with John Surtees and Willy Mairesse led most of the race until Willy had a fiery accident on Sunday morning and was hospitalised. Willy can be seen (lower right picture) in a leather coat and white overalls beyond the ramp.*

Dunlop's Vic Barlow checks tyre pressures.

Mechanics prepare the Parkes car for practice. 'Prova Mo 49' allows the car to be taken on to the public road. Although street legal, this was a racing car, pure and simple!

Phil Hill in discussion with his team. No 18 is the 4 litre Aston Martin 215P (prototype) Phil shared with Lucien Bianchi. Whilst a serious contender for victory, it was out of the race after two hours with a damaged gearbox, probably the result of running over accident debris.

The Innes Ireland and Bruce McLaren works 3.7 litre Aston Martin in the GT category, which was faster than the 215P in practice on the Mulsanne Straight. Ireland and McLaren lasted just over 4 hours into the race.

4 litre Ferrari 330 LM prototype entered by UK's Maranello Concessionaires for Jack Sears and Mike Salmon. The car was driven from the factory in Italy on trade plates by Col. Ronnie Hoare and finished the race in a worthy 5th place!

French privately-entered 4 litre Ferrari 330 LM prototype of Jean Guichet and Pierre Noblet, a long-term pairing in endurance events of the sixties. They retired from this race on Saturday evening. (The three semi-circular panels on the leading edge could be removed for extra cooling.) Only 4 of these Le Mans Berlinettas were built, including this French owned chassis 4381 here and chassis 4725 on page 128. These cars were essentially beefed up GTOs with arguably even prettier bodies!

The Ferraris and drivers assembling for practice. Mike Parkes has his crash helmet in a cardboard box. Behind is Ludovico Scarfiotti and, in the background, Mauro Forghieri and Eugenio Dragoni.

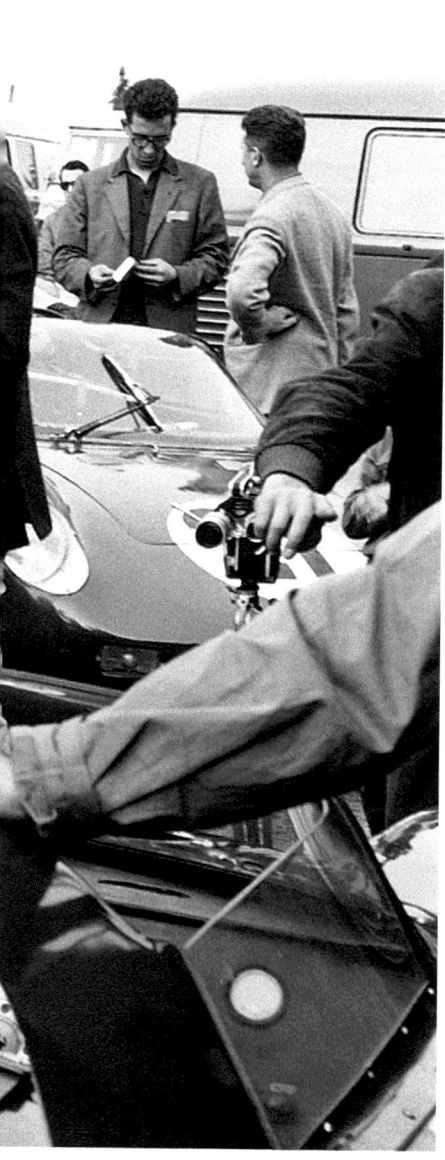

The three works Ferraris lined up in front of the pits for the start of practice. The eagle-eyed will identify numerous personalities here!

Phil Hill receives instructions from Aston Martin Team Manager John Wyer during practice. Mechanics clean the windscreen and check over the car. This overhead shot exemplifies the stunning lines of this Prototype class car, achieving 180mph (290kph) on the Mulsanne Straight. However, the team's 3.7 litre GTs were also very fast. This car is in safe hands today in the north of England.

Innes Ireland talks to Bruce McLaren, sitting in the cockpit. The team's similar car No 7 was driven by Bill Kimberly and Jo Schlesser and lasted rather longer than its team mates but was out of the race in the early hours of Sunday morning with engine failure. A dismal outing for the team!

A bearded Stirling Moss, fourteen months after his Goodwood accident, was managing the AC Cobra team on a one-off basis – here, interviewed on film.

Minutes before the start, Phil Hill chats to a photographer. Car No 2 is the 4.9 litre Maserati 151 driven by André Simon and American Lloyd Casner. It was fast but went out after three hours.

Winner Lorenzo Bandini signing autographs after the prizegiving ceremony. Together with Ludovico Scarfiotti and their Ferrari, they were the first all-Italian team to win Les Vingt Quatres Heures, completing 4562km at an average speed of 190kph. Ferraris filled the first six places!

23rd Jun 1963 — Dutch Grand Prix ZANDVOORT

Giancarlo Baghetti looking none too confident about his chances with the new ATS team, formed around a breakaway management group from Scuderia Ferrari. The team was backed by Italian businessmen, but the whole project was a disaster and had disappeared by the end of the year after missing numerous races.

Phil Hill led the ATS team but both cars failed in the race. Here, he talks to Dan Gurney who came second in a Brabham Climax V8 type BT7, driving alongside team boss Jack Brabham. The race was won by Jim Clark in a Lotus Climax V8 type 25.

Phil Hill's ATS V8 which qualified on the 5th row of a 'three-two-three' grid for 13th place, two ahead of Baghetti.

ATS Chief Engineer Carlo Chiti, here talking to Rob Walker (left). Chiti lost much credibility from the ATS experience but went on to work for Alfa Romeo and designed their F1 cars of the late 1970s.

| 7-8 July 2001 | **Festival of Speed GOODWOOD** |

Phil Hill (in glasses) adjusting the pedals of Chris Rea's replica Ferrari V6 type 156.

| 30th Jun 1963 | **French Grand Prix REIMS** |

Dick Protheroe, with his recognisable Jaguar E Type (CUT 7), came second to Carlo Abate's Ferrari Testa Rossa in the GT and Sports/Prototypes race which supported the Grand Prix.

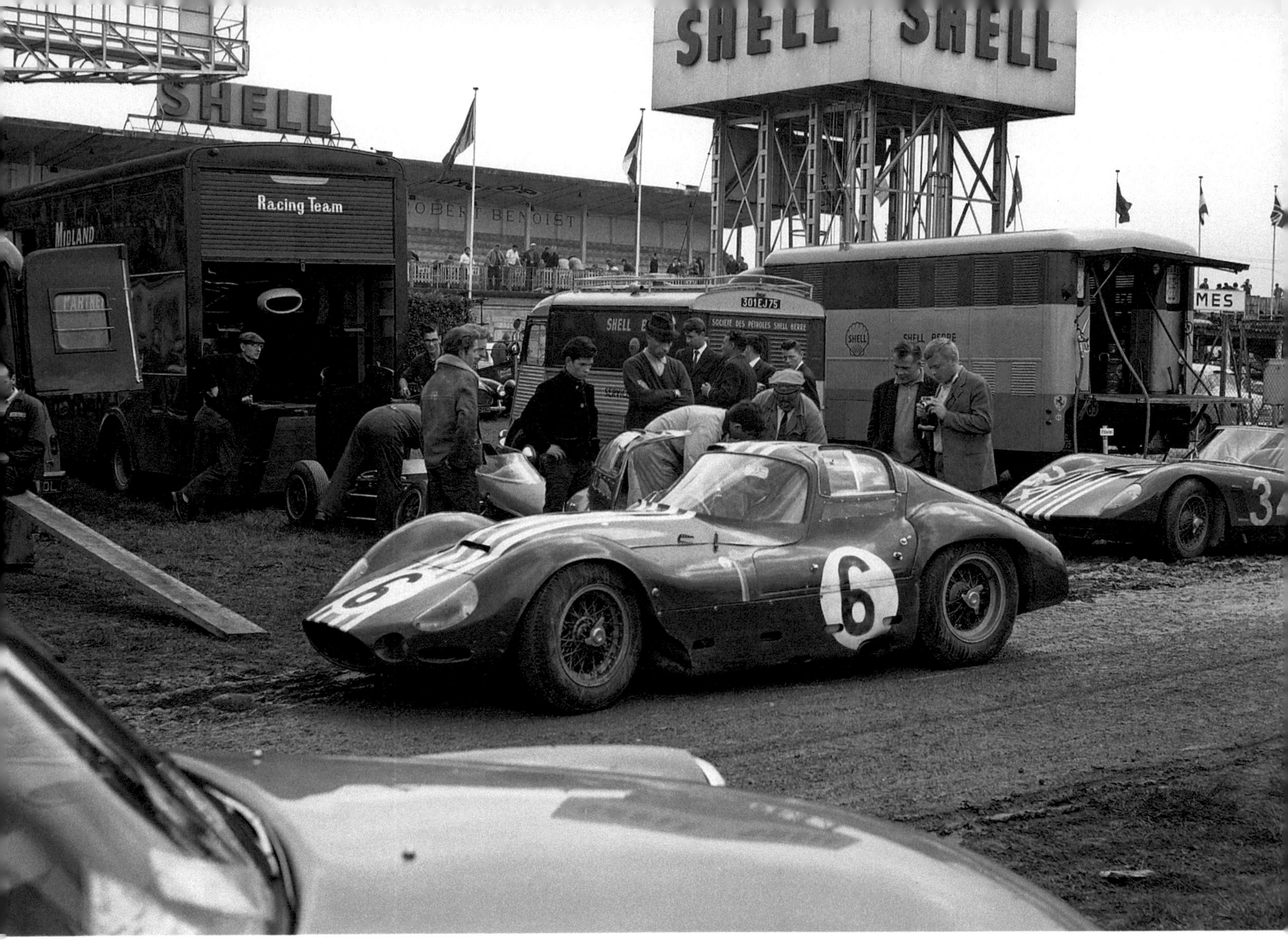

That 'beautifully ugly' Maserati 151, now with 4.9 litre V8 engine, first seen at Brands Hatch the previous year, and here driven by André Simon. Lloyd Casner can be seen in a feathered cap beside the big Maserati. He was driving car No 34, an elderly 3 litre Maserati type 61, which had a prettier body than the original 'birdcage', so called because of the myriad of small diameter tubing which formed the chassis and frame. Neither Maserati finished the race. Normand Racing (seen in the background) was a successful British entrant of Lotus 23s.

Many of the Prototypes, GT and Sports cars at Reims had come from Le Mans two weeks earlier, including this Aston Martin 215P, driven there by Phil Hill. Here it was driven by Jo Schlesser, but retired during the race, as did many of the top runners. Team Manager Reg Parnell, sporting a natty pair of shades, had a long career as a driver before he turned to team management, mostly with Aston Martin but also with The Bowmaker Yeoman Racing Team (see page 78).

Phil Hill settles into the brand new Lotus BRM V8 type 24 entered by Scuderia Filipinetti. In the absence of the ATS team, Hill was grateful for anything to drive, but this was not a success either as the car succumbed to clutch trouble.

A mechanic looks for John Surtees, the Formula 1 car beside the Ferrari 250P! Two F1 cars were entered for the Grand Prix but Scarfiotti crashed in practice and injured his legs.

Reims had substantial backing and could even boast these hospitality units! The little 760cc Renault 4CV (on right) was France's answer to the Volkswagon Beetle with over one million sold. Even the French police used them! Note the doors opening the 'wrong way'. Also in the picture are my two Danish companions who took me on "the slowest lap ever" of the Reims circuit in their dilapidated Volksbus (see page 57).

Mike Parkes chats with Jim Clark in the pit lane during practice, Colin Chapman being ushered out of the way by the arm of the law! The tail section of the Ferrari 250P is closed and Parkes pulls on his leather string-backed driving gloves ready for a fast lap, which equalled Jim Clark's pole time for the Grand Prix. Parkes had problems and was unclassified in the race. The 250P had a 4 litre V12 here instead of the 3 litre at Le Mans.

2001 Reims revisited

The old Reims circuit revisited in September 2001. The circuit was first used in 1925 and known as Reims-Gueux after the village through which it ran. That was bypassed for safety reasons from 1953 onwards. Note the old Total scoreboard and the mass of trees that have taken over the derelict paddock. The last French Grand Prix was held here in 1966, and the circuit finally closed in 1970; the facilities abandoned but not forgotten by anyone who remembers its history ... Revisited once more in 2006, a local group has been formed to restore the pits and grandstands, the site secured in perpetuity it would seem. An annual subscription of 20 euros is invited from anyone interested in helping to fund the work.

DUNLOP
TR BUNE JEAN- IERRE WIMILLE

Shell

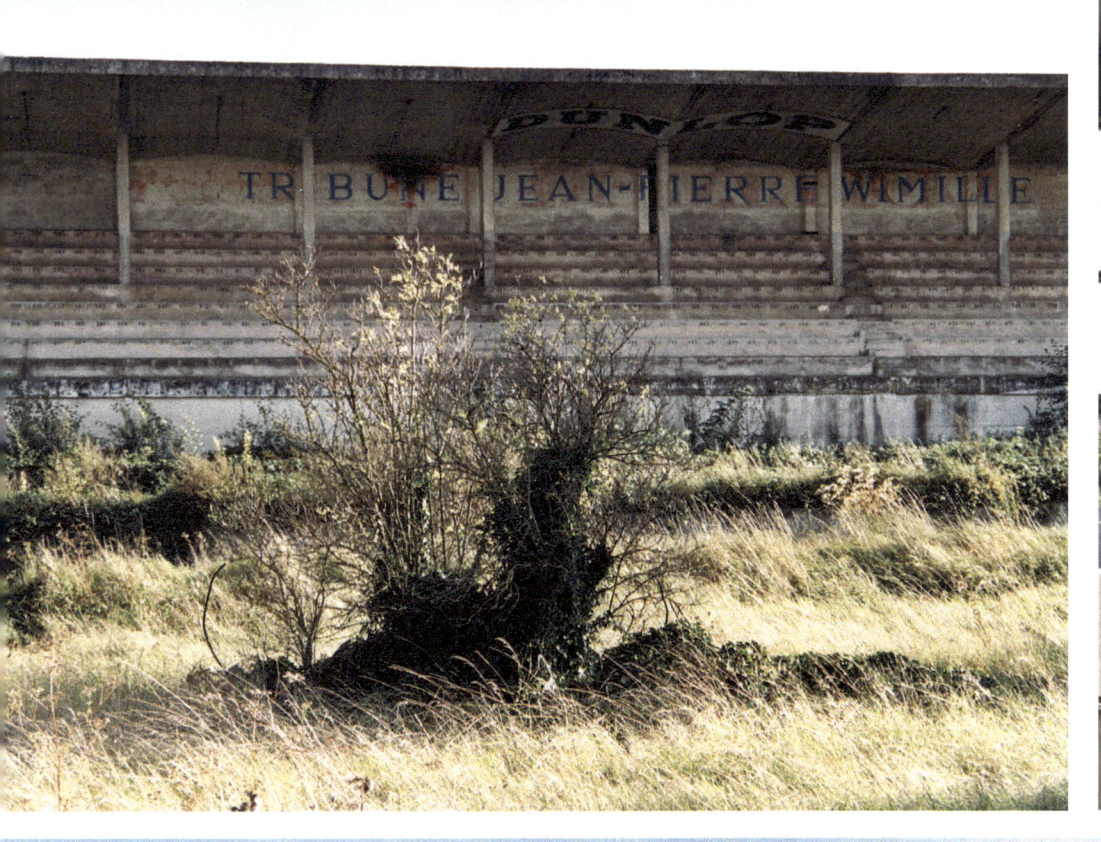

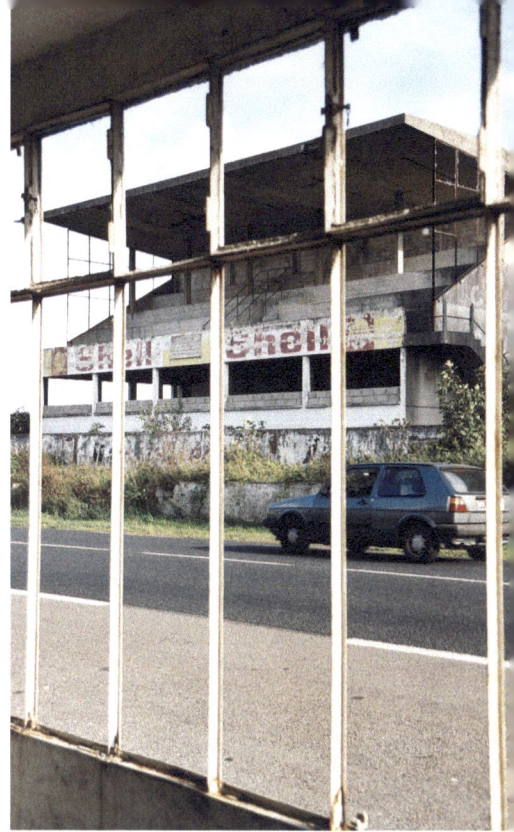

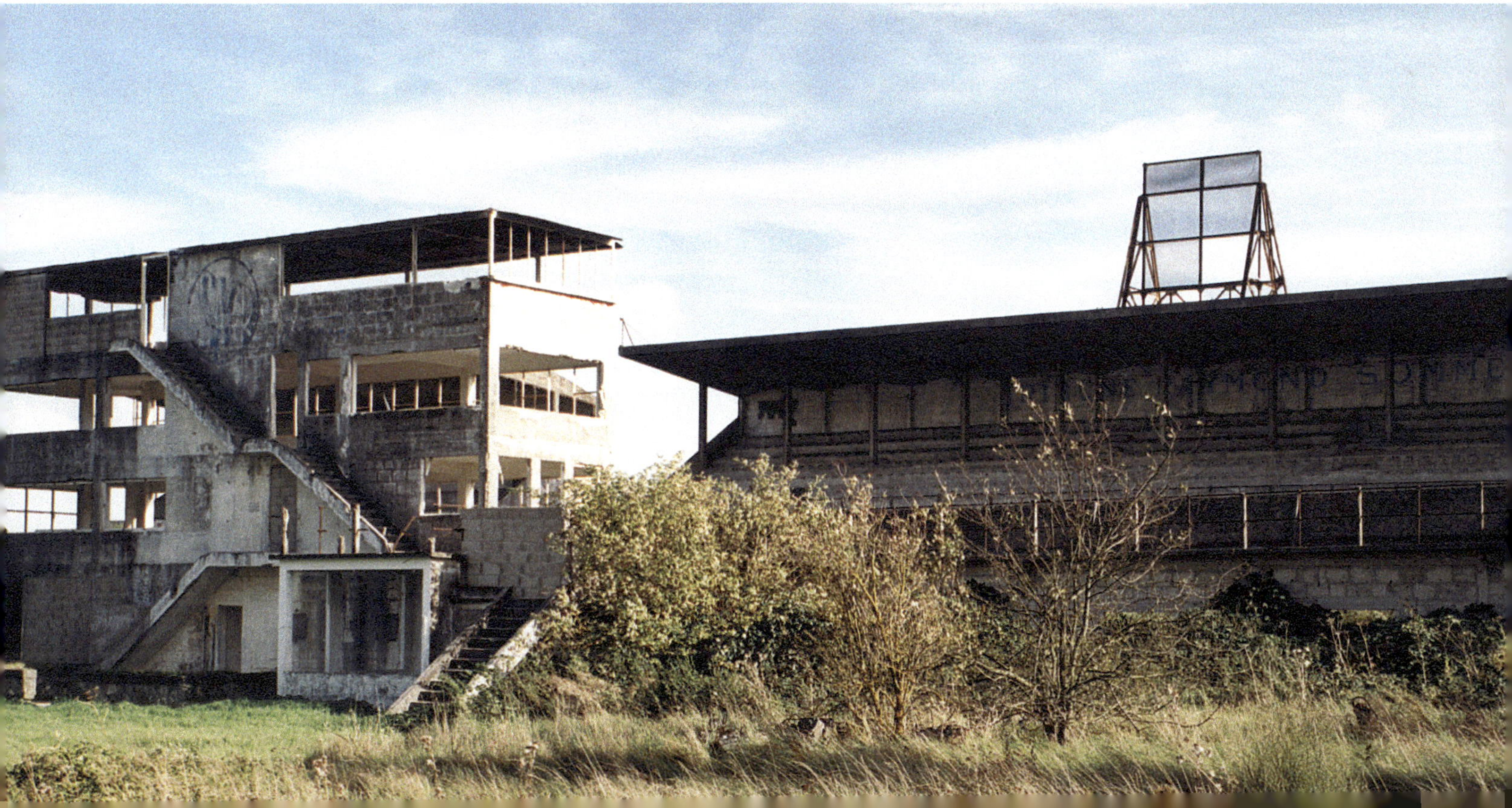

20th Jul 1963 — British Grand Prix SILVERSTONE

This neat Formula 1 car with a flat 8 cylinder engine was the de Tomaso, which arrived for practice but never turned a wheel. Occasional racer, Argentinian Alessandro de Tomaso, established his small factory in Modena in 1959, his fertile mind producing ideas which seldom achieved their potential. The entire car was of de Tomaso manufacture; note the strengthening detachable cross members above the engine, the latter fed by four Weber downdraught carburettors. Sadly, the project was stillborn.

The 7 litre Ford Galaxie entered by John Willment Automobiles for Jack Sears, here seen about to get into the car. The Galaxie was to transform saloon car racing – the great days of Jaguar domination at an end. 'Gentleman' Jack won the race, cruising round in top gear once he had disposed of the opposition!

Another Galaxie, this one the private entry of Sir Gawaine Baillie, arriving at the circuit. Sir Gawaine was another deserter from the Jaguar fold and finished 2nd here.

The dark blue diesel engined Ecurie Ecosse transporter built on a Commer 7 ton coach chassis by Walter Alexander of Falkirk. Corgi toys sold over 180,000 scale models. The team's Tojeiro-Buick is carried on the top deck. This transporter is often seen at historic events, now lovingly restored.

Why anyone would wish to rework the body of a Ferrari GTO is difficult to imagine but this was a pretty alternative, the work of Drogo and owned and driven by Chris Kerrison. It was not as successful as its looks might suggest.

147

American driver Augie Pabst raises the tail section of the Lola GT Ford V8 entered by Texan oil millionaire John Mecom, manually tweaking the throttle cable and instantly drawing a crowd around this exciting car. It retired early in the race with piston failure. Pabst was a wealthy amateur driver, well known in the States but hardly at all in Europe.

Early morning mist begins to clear on the North Downs as the teams prepare for practice. This works Aston Martin GT was driven by young pipe-smoking American Bill Kimberly (seen on the right in the photo on page 149). He spun out of the race at Dingle Dell.

John Wyer (centre) was one of the most respected team managers of his era, working variously with Aston Martin, and running the Mirages and Gulf Porsche 917s. Here, he listens to his driver Bill Kimberly (left) and rival Roy Salvadori, who was driving Tommy Atkins' Cooper Monaco Climax 2.7 litre, and finished 2nd in the Guards Trophy to Roger Penske in a Cooper derived Zerex Special.

16th Jul 1966 — **British Grand Prix BRANDS HATCH**

Family man Graham Hill holding daughter Samantha with Brigitte at his side.

Dan Gurney launched his Anglo American Racers in 1966, building the Eagle but using an out of date Coventry Climax 4 cylinder 2.7 litre engine, pending availability of his V12. Dan qualified well on the front row, but the old engine let him down in the race.

Once again Britain was unprepared for the new Formula 1 – 3 litres from 1966. With BRM's ambitious H16 still unreliable, the team used the 2 litre 'Tasman' V8 in the old P261 chassis seen here. BRM was short of these 'obsolete' cars, Stewart's having been wrecked at Spa, so the team had to recover one already sold and on exhibition in Japan for him to drive here. Seen here are Chief Mechanic Alan Challis and Denis Perkins, in charge of gearboxes (right). This was Graham Hill's car which finished third behind two Brabhams.

Jochen Rindt looks despondent about his prospects with Cooper, talking here to Roy Salvadori – now managing the Cooper team.

Bruce McLaren was another driver having a torrid time with his own new Formula 1 team. He was using a new 3 litre Serenissima V8 and though he finished 6th here, elsewhere the car was unsuccessful. Unusually, this first Formula 1 McLaren (M2B) had a Malite 'sandwich' monocoque construction.

Cooper used this heavy Maserati V12 throughout 1966 for hard-worked drivers John Surtees (recently having parted company from Ferrari), and Jochen Rindt, who finished 5th. Surtees coped with deteriorating handling before having to retire.

29th Aug 1966 — International Guards Trophy Meeting **BRANDS HATCH**

The 'business end' of Chris Amon's brutish McLaren-Elva, with Tyler Alexander (still with McLaren in the 21st century!) checking the tyres. These early cars were built under licence by Elva.

Twenty-three year old New Zealander Chris Amon was fast carving a name for himself, here driving a McLaren-Elva Chevrolet V8 with team boss Bruce in the other car. Chris seemed all set for a Formula 1 career with the McLaren team, and caused some ill-feeling when he signed with Ferrari for 1967.

John Surtees in his Team Surtees Ltd Lola T70 MkII giving mechanic Malcolm Malone a lift down to the pits. The Guards Trophy was run in two heats; the second was stopped during torrential rain and re-run over a shortened distance. Surtees won overall, Amon came second and Bruce McLaren slid off the road!

Opposite: John Surtees with John Webb, Managing Director Brands Hatch Circuits Ltd, and Lola's Eric Broadley (left).

The cockpit of Mike Salmon's Ford GT 40 which finished 2nd in the Group 4 Sports Car race to David Piper's new Ferrari 275 LM.

The pristine white Lola T70 Chevrolet V8 of private entrant Sid Taylor, a very successful car, invariably driven by Denny Hulme. It had an off day here.

The Ferrari 250 LM of owner/driver Ron Fry. Ron never got into the big time, he just loved driving his Ferrari.

AC Cobras waiting to go down to the pits for practice. Registration 'LOV 1' on the right was entered by The Chequered Flag team.

Peter Arundell's Team Lotus Cortina which finished 3rd in the Edward Lewis Shoes Trophy for Saloon Cars.

Jim Clark, here talking to Team Lotus Chief Mechanic Bob Dance, was driving the other Lotus Cortina with the BRM-developed engine (top right). Bob had a long career, later working with Mario Andretti and Ronnie Peterson and nowadays can often be seen at historic meetings looking after the cars for Classic Team Lotus. BRM had gained a fine reputation for the development of engines as a separate business in support of its Grand Prix team.

Jim gives a young passenger a lift down to the pits. Jim was astonishing to watch in these cars, he just revelled in three and even two wheel cornering! He won, of course!

| June 1967 | **Ferrari Factory, Maranello** |

Through the archway: the sprayed panels of 330 P4s were drying in the afternoon sun outside the racing department. The two of us were given an extensive tour of the factory by our guide, Signor Alfredo Vassalo – so much more detailed than would have been possible with a large party.

The Ferrari 330 P4 V12 being fuelled ready to run around the courtyard, prior to being handed over to Equipe Nationale Belge where it was driven into 3rd place at Le Mans by Willy Mairesse and 'Beurlys' (also pages 162/163). Note the 'petrolio' being filtered through a chamois leather!

Bodies of 275 GTB/4s (350 built, 27 with UK RHD, launch price £6516) and 365 Californias (14 built, 2 with UK RHD, launch price £9220) waiting on trestles before proceeding to the production line for installation of engines, running gear, etc.

The foundry, machining (previous page) and engine assembly departments (above) seen on a Saturday afternoon with the the occasional engineer at work.

Completed 330 GTCs coming off the production line. Protective fibreglass shrouds cover the wings. 600 of these cars were built, 21 of them with UK RHD, launch price £6516.

1995 Ferrari Factory, Maranello

Spot the differences between this photo of the famous entrance taken in 1995 and that taken in 1967 (page 64). The racing department is now located in the Via Ascari, half a mile away. In 1995 I watched qualifying for Barcelona on a big screen television in the Ferrari reception office, the staff going crazy as Jean Alesi took pole position for a while in the type 412/T2.

7th Jul 1968 — French Grand Prix
ROUEN-LES-ESSARTS

After a disastrous two year start with his fledgling Formula 1 team – even driving Dan Gurney's Eagles for a time in 1967 – Bruce McLaren was right on target from the beginning of 1968 with wins in two non-championship races. Here he tries the cockpit of his McLaren M7A, powered by the ubiquitous Ford-Cosworth V8 DFV engine which spawned new teams with this 'customer' engine taking over from where Coventry Climax left off. Note the rear wing mounted on the engine cam covers; such aerodynamic devices were in their infancy at this time. The McLaren team finished second in the Constructor's Championship with three victories. A remarkable result.

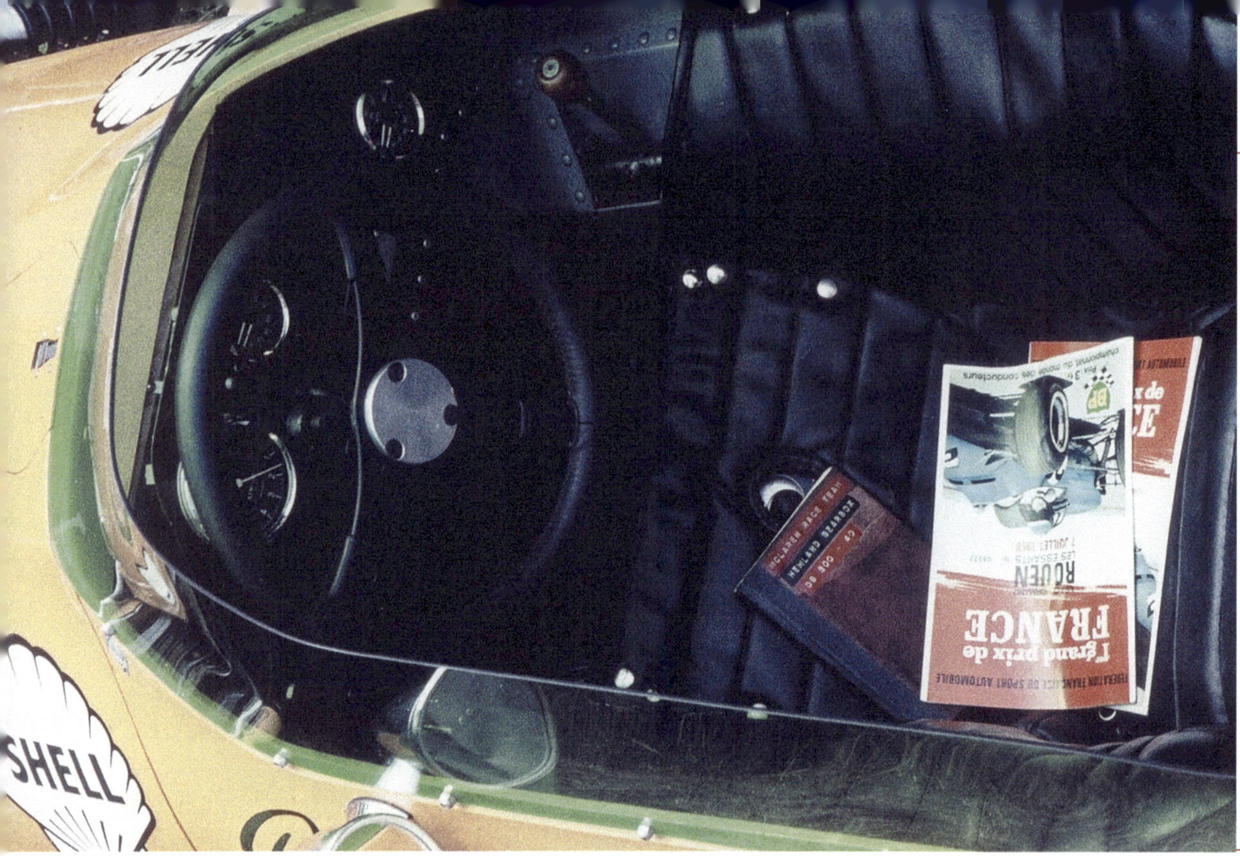

Oh! for the days when company secrets could be left lying about! The oil-stained note book is entitled McLaren Race Team – Hewland Gearbox.

Fellow Kiwi Denny Hulme joined McLaren from Brabham for 1968. Here he is with Goodyear's Phil Kerr, turning the pages of a new book, this picture depicting the start of a 12 hours Sebring race.

"What's he up to?" seems to be the question in Bruce's mind as he watches Tyler Alexander working on the front of the car.

John Surtees' Honda V12 type RA301, the chassis developed by Lola at Slough and irreverently referred to as the 'Hondola'! Designer Yoshio Nakamura blasts the ears of onlookers as he fires up the engine.

The team's other Honda was the brand new RA302 with air-cooled V8 engine. It had arrived in England a week earlier from Japan for Surtees to test. "What looks right is right" is a useful rule of thumb, and this car looked all wrong! French driver Jo Schlesser died in a fiery accident when he lost control of the ill-handling car in wet race day conditions.

'Big John' concentrated on the RA301 (below) and finished in an unexpected 2nd place after retiring from the previous three races. Here the discussion seems to revolve around braking! Surtees is on the right.

Above: Primitive working conditions, kit everywhere, the cockpit covered in case of showers. A typical paddock of the period: "... just a clearing in the forest." Richard Attwood finished 7th and Pedro Rodriguez, with gearbox selection problems, was unclassified. Tim Parnell, BRM's Team Manager (facing) and Denis Perkins (right). The V12 engine was brought into service following the disappointment of the H16 in 1967.

The Ferraris were type 312 V12s; two cars for Chris Amon, the lead driver, and No 26 for Jacky Ickx.

Ferrari arrived at Rouen with this magnificent purpose-built transporter, the envy of the paddock. The familiar open deck transporter Ferrari had used for years was put away – well, almost!

"... one of the bravest and the fastest ...". Though he failed to win a single World Championship Grand Prix, Chris Amon is remembered as one of the great drivers of his era, making an incalculable contribution to Ferrari during one of its most difficult periods. Italian hero Lorenzo Bandini died at Monaco in 1967, Mike Parkes crashed out of racing the same year, and Chris Amon was left to carry Ferrari almost single-handedly for the remainder of that terrible year, his first with the team. The cars were not the best and Chris moved on at the end of 1969, just as Ferrari was about to begin a rennaisance.

That glorious V12 sound transmitted by those spaghetti exhausts lives on. Note the aerofoil mounted directly onto the engine; the first year these devices were used in Formula 1.

Amon was uncertain about the supposed advantage the aerofoil had given him at Spa a month earlier. For France, 'wings' were all the rage, and experimentation rife! One thing was certain, it provided a useful work bench!

"Jacky Ickx was inspirational to watch in any car and wet conditions were his forte". His first full year in Formula 1, twenty-three years old and Ferrari a challenging environment, even for the toughest! Jacky had this race in the bag from the moment he opted for 'wet' tyres on the grid, the only driver to do so. He won at a canter and his reputation was established. Amon was on dry weather tyres and finished five laps behind.

The Cooper BRM V12s type 86B looked very 'traditional' here, wearing no hint of advertising and leaving the bigger teams to do the pioneering work on aerofoils. Vic Elford (No 30) finished a worthy 4th in his first Grand Prix, while French heartthrob Johny Servoz-Gavin went off into the woods in the miserable conditions. Cooper's switch from Maserati V12 to BRM V12 failed to bring it any more success. The team dropped from third in the Constructors Championship with 28 points in 1967 to sixth place in 1968 with 14 points. It was its last year as a works team, a sad ending for a marque which created the rear-engined revolution and won World Championships in 1959 and 1960 with Jack Brabham.

Jackie Oliver had a terrible accident in this Lotus 49B in final practice. He was uninjured, but his car was written-off, so failed to take the start on Sunday. Note the tall wing: designers delving into the realms of the unknown with these new aeronautical devices.

Jack Brabham. World Championships secured for Brabham drivers and cars in 1966 and 1967, but struggling in 1968 with only one finish for his cars in the first five races. The Brabham Repco V8 type BT26 (below): note the mounting of the wing support.

"... like a boy with a new skateboard ..." Jochen Rindt was ecstatic about the sudden form of his new Brabham Repco V8 type BT26, achieving pole position in first practice. Denny Hulme studies his old team's car.

Colin Chapman wearing Gold Leaf corporate colours – an early indication of the impact of sponsorship.

Aerofoils/wings came in all shapes and sizes. It's difficult to believe that Jean-Pierre Beltoise achieved very much with this offering on the Matra V12 type MS11.

All ready for practice. Plenty to pick out in this photo, including a Franciscan friar! Graham Hill is in his familiar helmet (London Rowing Club colours) and Bette is on the pit counter ready for lap timing. Jacky Ickx is helmeted and ready to go in the Ferrari pit and Jo Siffert sits in Rob Walker's dark blue Lotus 49.

1999 Rouen-les-Essarts, revisited

"... the main grandstand ... would have been more in keeping at Mallory Park". The sad relics of Rouen-les-Essarts, once a great circuit, here photographed in 1999. Revisited in September 2004, all the facilities at the circuit had disappeared, leaving no sign of the circuit's former glory. Even the pillar into which Jackie Oliver crashed has been demolished. Curiously, the nearby bus stop is labelled Circuit Auto. The place deserves a better memorial ... The French Grand Prix was last held here in 1968.

THE SEQUEL

So the sixties gave way to the next decade, too recent a memory to justify detailed comment here. There were the Lauda years at Ferrari which restored the *Scuderia* to the front line, and secured both Driver's and Constructor's Championships in 1975 and 1977. There was the emergence of Gilles Villeneuve, whose memory will live forever and who was my son's great hero just as mine had been Juan Manuel Fangio twenty years earlier. It was the decade when 'slicks' were introduced; of enormous strides in safety; the unique six-wheeled Tyrrell; ground effects; the Brabham fan car, and the first win by a turbo-engined car in 1979. For the rest, let the pictures tell their own story.

The sixties was a pivotal decade. So many events took place which changed the face of motor racing in general and Grand Prix in particular. We saw the end of the front engined car; the introduction of the monocoque; sponsorship which began a new visual impact; aerodynamic aids and four-wheel-drive, the latter a brief and abandoned experiment. We remember John Surtees as the first man to win World Championships on four wheels as well as two, and Jim Clark and Lotus invading the 'brickyard' to win the Indianapolis 500. Last but not least there was the Ford-Cosworth V8 DFV, the most successful Grand Prix engine ever!

Sir Jackie Stewart says his times in racing were not the 'good old days' but the 'bad old days'; the result, surely, of remembering so many lost friends and the frustration of constantly striving for advances in safety. One thing is certain: our sport is now immeasurably safer, immeasurably better organised and, as always, breaking through technological barriers. Whether or not it is still fun is something I must leave readers to decide for themselves ...

The John Player Special Lotus Cosworth V8 type 72 of Emerson Fittipaldi who retired on the third lap. The JPS was surely one of the best-looking car/corporate sponsorship combinations ever. Note the bearded John Watson (left). Race of Champions, Brands Hatch, 1973.

18th Mar 1973 — Race of Champions, BRANDS HATCH

Denny Hulme preparing to go out for practice in the McLaren Cosworth V8 type M23, one of the marque's most successful cars. The race was padded out with 20 Formula 5000 cars to produce a mixed field of 36. A Formula 5000 car won against Formula 1 for the first time in England – Peter Gethin in a Chevron B24 Chevrolet V8. Hulme was 2nd.

Jean-Pierre Beltoise and the BRM P160 V12 which finished 6th. Beltoise secured BRM's last World Championship race win – the Monaco GP, 1972. Sadly, by now the team was in serious decline.

1973 14th Jul — British Grand Prix
SILVERSTONE

The monocoque of the Ferrari 312 B3 flat 12-engined car was constructed in England by specialist John Thompson because of industrial unrest in Italy. The car was not a success and 1973 was one of the all-time 'lows' in Ferrari's history. Jacky Ickx finished 8th here and left the team later in the season, leaving Arturo Merzario to soldier on as best he could.

1974 20th Jul — British Grand Prix
BRANDS HATCH

The seemingly large Tyrrell Cosworth V8 type 007s of Patrick Depailler and Jody Scheckter. The cars looked clean and uncluttered with just two major sponsors. Jody won two championship races, including this one, and with Tyrrell finished 3rd in their respective championships.

Jacky Ickx was hoping to re-ignite his career with JPS Lotus, but it was not to be. Apart from winning the non-championship Race of Champions in the wet (and what a spectacle that was), Jacky's Formula 1 career just walked away from him and he left Lotus mid-1975 after a number of car failures which destroyed his confidence. In Sports cars it was another matter, of course ...

The casual appearance of Ronnie Peterson belied an extraordinary talent, and no-one who saw him would forget his awesome speed. He mastered the old type '72' with victories in three championship races in 1974, but, sadly, died following a start line accident at Monza in 1978, still with JPS Lotus. Here at Brands Hatch he started from the outside of the front row but was out of luck in the race (finishing tenth), his team mate (above) having an untypically good race and finishing third.

After an appalling season in 1973, Ferrari was back on course for 1974 with Chief Engineer Mauro Forghieri working closely with new signing Niki Lauda, the whole team overseen by Luca di Montezemolo. The car was an improved type 312 B3, built entirely at Maranello. Involvement with endurance racing ended after many years so that the team's focus was now entirely on Formula 1. How we miss those Sports Prototypes ...

Mauro Forghieri in earnest conversation with Goodyear's technician, whilst a young-looking di Montezemolo seems to be contemplating the team's tactics!

Giulio Borsari checks over a replacement flat 12 to be installed for race day.

Veteran Ferrari Chief Mechanic Giulio Borsari whom I had seen around for years.

Rugged Swiss ace Gianclaudio 'Clay' Regazzoni was Ferrari's kind of driver: tough and committed to the Ferrari cause. He had been with the team for three years, but went to BRM for 1973 when it became clear that Ferrari was in the doldrums and might have the resources to run only one car. He returned for the 'glory years' with Niki Lauda, 1974-1976, but, sadly, his long career in Formula 1 ended at Long Beach in 1980 when he hit the wall in an Ensign Cosworth and suffered severe leg injuries. He was confined to a wheel chair for the rest of his life but competed occasionally in cars adapted with hand controls. Sadly his luck ran out when he died in an accident on the Italian autostrada late in 2006.

The Ferrari's ancestry with the 1973 'Thompson B3' is easy to see, but in fact it was a very different car and the flat 12 engine much more powerful, with improved torque. The team had three victories in 1974 and Regazzoni and Ferrari were second in their respective championships. What a difference a year can make! Here Lauda started the race on pole but finished fifth, beaten by his team mate in fourth place.

Ermano Cuoghi, Lauda's personal mechanic, brought into the team at his insistence. Ermano had worked on the Gulf Porsche 917s managed by John Wyer.

A trestle table, a few chairs and an awning gave the teams much needed civilised conditions, and spectators could still see what was going on. Niki Lauda (right) in joking mood whilst Forghieri and di Montezemolo try to ignore him!

Now we know what those side pods were for! Emerson Fittipaldi finished second in the race in one of these Marlboro Team Texaco McLaren M23s – he and McLaren winning the 1974 championships.

Embassy Racing with Graham Hill ran Lola Cosworth V8 type 370s to extend this great driver's career, but he was killed in a flying accident in November 1975, just when his team had ambitious plans for the future. Tony Brise, his young star driver, died in the same accident. Hill finished 13th at Brands.

Bernie Ecclestone bought out the Brabham team (Motor Racing Developments) in 1972, but these virgin white Cosworth engined BT44s seem in need of a sponsor! Curiously, they were lined up in front of 'Uncle Ken's' transporter! Carlos Reutemann (No 7) and Carlos Pace finished 6th and 9th respectively.

The 12 cylinder engine was almost Enzo Ferrari's raison d'être, whether in V12 or flat 12 form. What would he make of the modern V10s revving to 19,000rpm? Regazzoni finished 4th here (No 11) and Lauda 5th.

14th Jul 1979 — British Grand Prix SILVERSTONE

Jody Scheckter became World Champion and Ferrari won the Constructor's title in 1979. Throughout, Jody received loyal support from team-mate Gilles Villeneuve who finished second in the title race, four points behind. By this time Jody was one of Formula 1's elder statesmen, so different from the 'rock ape' image of 1973 when he caused a first lap multi pile-up at Silverstone's Woodcote Corner!

Gilles Villeneuve's flat 12 engined Ferrari 312 T4 minus the front wing. My regret is that there is no photograph of him here. Jody finished 5th in this race and Gilles retired in the closing stages with fuel vaporisation, but was classified 14th.

The car that changed Formula 1! Renault took a low-key approach initially, working away quietly with the turbo-engined car with just one entry for Jean-Pierre Jabouille. For 1979 Renault had a two car (the RS10) team which included René Arnoux, and it was only fitting that Jabouille scored the team's first victory at Dijon in the French GP. It was there that Villeneuve and Arnoux had their unforgettable wheel-bashing duel for second place, the former ahead at the finish. Here at Silverstone Arnoux was 2nd and Jabouille retired early.

Miscellaneous memorabilia

Programme for the German Grand Prix, 1956.

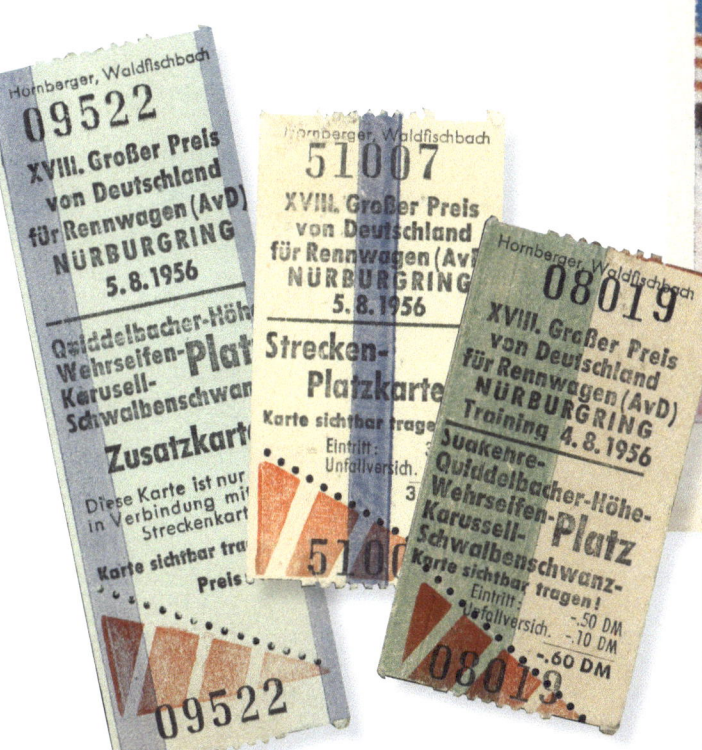

Admission tickets for the German GP, 1956. One for 'training 4th August, 1956', one for 'Strecken Platzkarte 5th August, 1956' and one for admission to the 'Karusell Platz 5th August, 1956'.

Les Grands Prix de Reims 1963
Programme Officiel : 2 F.

Curiously, this programme cover omits to refer to the race as the French Grand Prix!

MARANELLO CONCESSIONAIRES LTD
CHAIRMAN COL R J HOARE CBE   DIRECTORS G L DIPPEY D C MACLEOD
WELLESLEY ROAD · LONDON · W4
TELEPHONE CHISWICK 4928

RJH/LJ.

18th January 1967.

A. F. Carter, Esq.,
Oldbury House,
Ightham,
Sevenoaks,
Kent.

Dear Sir,

We thank you for your letter dated 18th January 1967. Arrangements can be made for an organized visit to the Ferrari factory at Maranello, Italy. These take place on Saturday afternoons only at 2 p.m.

In making your arrangements you should avoid the first fortnight of August and the first two weeks of September. The factory is closed during the former period and factory visits are not allowed during the latter owing to security arrangements prior to the Italian Grand Prix.

If you could be kind enough to let us know the date you wish to visit the factory and the number to be included in your party, we shall be only too pleased to make the necessary arrangements for you.

Yours faithfully,
MARANELLO CONCESSIONAIRES.LTD.

R. J. Hoare.
Chairman.

ferrari
SOLE CONCESSIONAIRES
GREAT BRITAIN, NORTHERN IRELAND AND EIRE

Letter from Col. R. J. Hoare, Chairman Maranello Concessionaires concerning my visit to the Ferrari factory in 1967.

Grazie e cordiali saluti
Ferrari

> A faded message from Enzo Ferrari, in the familiar violet ink, in response to my letter of congratulation on his new successes in 1974: 'Grazie e cordiale salute', signed E. Ferrari.

[signature: Ronnie Peterson]

Modena, 8 agosto 1974

 Clay Regazzoni

STIRLING MOSS

TELEPHONE: FULHAM 1106
PLEASE REPLY TO
MANAGER: KENNETH GREGORY

8 CHALLONER MANSIONS
WEST KENSINGTON
LONDON W.14

DATE 16th October, 1953

J. Newman, Esq.,
Blackfriars School,
Laxton,
Corby,
Northants.

Dear John and Anthony,

Stirling has asked me to reply to your very kind and interesting letter of the 10th October, and to thank you for your very kind wishes and regards.

I am pleased to say that he is now well on the way to a complete recovery, his main injury being a broken right arm which prevents him from attending to his correspondence.

In closing, he has asked me to pass on his very kind regards to you both, and the hope that you will enjoy watching motor racing next year.

Yours sincerely,

K. A. Gregory
Manager

> Lastly: a letter from Ken Gregory, Stirling Moss' manager, following the boss's accident at Castle Coombe in October 1953.

10th Jul 1965 — British Grand Prix SILVERSTONE

These photographs, taken by Adrian Bromley, are included as a tribute to my great friend and fellow enthusiast, who accompanied me to so many of the races.

Ferrari used to have its cars flown over for the races in England, SS & Co traditionally transporting the cars and equipment to and from Heathrow. Whenever I see this company's trucks on the road today I instantly recall the Ferraris being gently eased down wooden planks, chocks placed beneath the wheels to raise the cars over the edge of the flatdeck. There were two V8s (type 158), plus a flat 12 engined car (1512) for John Surtees, in which he finished 3rd in the race, bearing No 1 as the current World Champion. Lorenzo Bandini's race lasted a mere two laps when he missed a gear and blew the engine! Beside the car in which Bandini is standing is a young apprentice mechanic around whom Shell created a lot of advertising at the time. In 2005 he was still working at Maranello, building Ferrari Formula 1 engines.

BRM's spare was an updated 1964 car.

Graham Hill with the BRMs, here talking to Col. Ronnie Hoare of Maranello Concessionaires. Jim Clark and Graham Hill were the pace setters in 1965, with young Jackie Stewart keeping them on their toes in the second BRM. Clark won in Britain for the fourth successive year in a Lotus Climax V8 type 33, with Hill second in the BRM V8 type 261. Stewart was 5th.

Also in the Veloce *Classic Reprints* Series:

Autodrome: The Lost Race Circuits of Europe
ISBN: 978-1-787111-29-5

Around Europe lie a number of long forgotten monuments, windswept and abandoned, the derelict buildings and crumbling tarmac are all that remain of once great motor racing circuits. From the great speed-bowls of Monza and Brooklands, to the parkland of Crystal Palace, this evocative book features both historical pictures, as well as stunning contemporary photography of the circuits as they are now.

Ford GT: Then & Now
ISBN: 978-1-787111-26-4

This book provides a different view of the Ford GT legend, featuring driver interviews, and both historical and new photographic records. Some of the old myths and legends of the racetrack have been revisited, Ford GT drivers have been given their place on the roll of honour, and their opponents on the racing track are also discussed. With details of the Ford GT replica industry, this book is an historical and interesting record of this classic car, and a must for all GT enthusiasts.

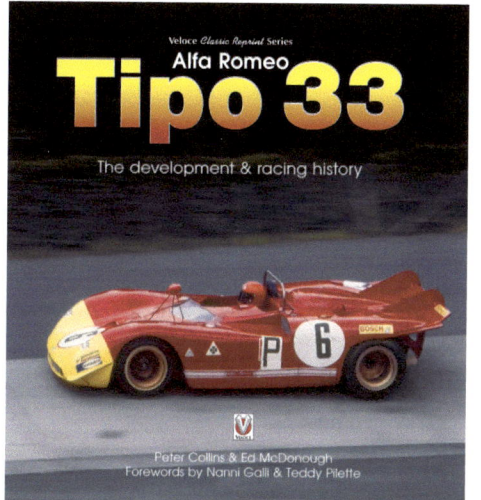

Alfa Romeo Tipo 33: The Development & Racing History
ISBN: 978-1-787111-31-8

At the time, little was recorded about the activities of Alfa Romeo's World Championship-winning Sports Racing car, the Tipo 33. The model had a long career, as a factory car as well as in private hands from 1967 until 1977. The great Italian motor sport engineer Carlo Chiti designed and ran a prolific number of different models of this Tipo. Unfortunately nothing of the history of these developments was documented at the time, but the authors have managed, after intense investigation and numerous personal interviews, to uncover much about this marvellous sports prototype. With many previously unseen photographs and interviews with key personalities, this is a vital addition to any Alfa enthusiasts collection.

For more information and price details, visit our website at www.veloce.co.uk
• email: info@veloce.co.uk • Tel: +44(0)1305 260068

Index

Bold entries denote photographs

305th Bomb Group 13, 59

Abate, Carlo 58, **105, 137**
AC Cobra **133, 157**
Adenau 9, 10, **26, 27,** 60
Agnelli, Giovanni 51
Aintree 15–17, 42, 44, 48
Aitken, Sir Max **28, 29**
AJS 23
Alboreto, Michele 63
Alesi, Jean **165**
Alexander, Tyler **154, 169**
Aley, John **111**
Alfa Romeo 11, 14, 15, **83**, 158
Alfa Romeo type 159 11
Allison, Cliff **72, 73, 76**
Alvis 49
AMC 23
American Air Force 13
American Grand Prix 42, 61
Amon, Chris 52, 57, 67, **154, 173, 174, 176**
Anglo American Racers 48
Ardennes 19
Argentina 10, 11, 22
Armstrong Siddeley Hurricane Drophead Coupé 13
Armstrong Siddeley Sixteen-Six 12, 13
Arnoux, René **196**
Arundel, Peter **157**
Ascari, Alberto 9, 15, 45, 56, 63
Aston 53
Aston Martin 20, 23, 58
Aston Martin DBR 4/250 **75**
Aston Martin 215 53
Aston Martin 215P **127, 139**
Aston Martin 215P 57
Aston Martin DB3S 20, **36**
Aston Martin DBR 1/300 20, 23, **33, 35, 74**
Aston Martin GT **128, 150**
Aston Martin Zagato 49, 60
Atkins, Cyril **84, 113**
Atkins, Tommy **81, 86, 150**
Atkinson Morley Hospital 44
ATS 54, 55, 57, **135, 136,** 141
Attwood, Richard 53, **123, 172**
Austin Lodestar **70**
Austrian Grand Prix 55
Auto Union 9

Autocar 42
Automobile Club de l'Ouest 52
Automóvil Club Argentino 10
Autosport 20
Avus 18

Baghetti, Giancarlo 42, 45, 54, 55, **135, 136**
Baillie, Sir Gawaine **147**
Bandini, Lorenzo 19, 53, 63, **115, 124, 134, 174, 201**
BAOR 9
Barcelona 65
Barlow, Vic **89, 126**
Barnett, Francis 23
Baxter, Raymond 19
BBC 64
Beaverbrook Newspapers **28**
Behra, Jean 17, 18, **18, 29, 33**
Belgian Grand Prix 16, 19, 48, 50, 51, **80**
Beltoise, J-P 18, 68, **69, 180, 183**
Berlin 18
Berlinetta 49
Berthon, Peter 43
Beurlys **161**
Bianchi, Lucien **40, 101, 127**
Bielefeld 9, 10
Bira, Prince 56
Blackbushe 59
Blumer, Jimmy **110**
BOAC 500 21, 55
Boddy, Bill 15
Boeing B17 13
Bologna 57
Bondurant, Bob 19
Bonnier, Jo 9, 47, **33, 81, 102**
Bordeaux 9
Border Reivers 21, **74**
Borsari, Giulio **188, 189**
Bourne 9, 16, 18
Bowmaker Yeoman Racing Team 45, **78, 89**
BP 44
Brabham 60, 182
Brabham BT26 66
Brabham Cosworth V8 BT44 **194**
Brabham Repco V8 BT26 **178, 179**
Brabham type BT7 55
Brabham, Jack 43, 46, 55, 61, 62, 67, **72, 92, 135, 178**

Braham Climax BT7 **135**
Brands Hatch 20–22, 44, 49, 55, 60, 61, 66, **100, 109, 139, 151, 154, 182, 183, 184**
BRDC 44, **29**
Brighton Speed Trials 59
Brise, Tony **193**
British Automobile Racing Club 51
British Drag Festival 59
British Grand Prix 15, 17, **41,** 42, 44, 48, 57, **146, 151, 184, 195, 200**
British Hill Climb Championship 20
British Medical Association 12
British Motor Racing Research Trust 16
British Racing & Sports Car Club (BRSCC) 20, 22
BRM 16–19, 22, **29,** 42, 43, 46, 48, 52, 53, 57, 58, 60, 61, 64–66, 68, **90, 91, 99, 113, 114, 122, 189**
BRM H16 18, 61, 66, **152, 172**
BRM P48 **70**
BRM P261 **152**
BRM P578 **84, 91, 115**
BRM type 25 17
BRM type 57 42
BRM type P160B 18
BRM type P207 18
BRM V12 68, **172**
BRM V12 P160 **183**
BRM V16 9, 15, 16
BRM V8 45, 61, **79, 80, 87, 152**
BRM V8 261 **202**
Broadley, Eric 53, 61, 67, **123, 155**
Brockbank, Russell 42
Brooke Bond Oxo 64
Brooks, Tony 15–17
Brown, Alan 15
Brown, David 23
Brussels 44
Bryden-Brown, Louise **77**
Bugatti 31
Burgess, Ian **93**
Burt, Patsy 20

Caen 17
Can Am 61
Carvath, Pat **79, 91, 99, 114**
Casablanca 16, 44
Casner, Lloyd **134, 139**
Castelotti, Eugenio 45, 63
Challis, Allan **152**

204

Chaparral Chevrolet 56
Chaparrel 55
Chapman, Colin 16, 21, 43, 58, 61, 62, 64, 66, 68, **100, 142, 179**
Chelveston 13, 59
Chequered Flag, The **74**
Chevrolet Specials 10
Chevron B24 **183**
Chichester 43
Chiti, Carlo 54, **136**
Christies 18
Christmas, Don 20
Clark, Jim 20, 21, 22, 42, 43, 45-47, 49, 51, 52, 55, 59, 60-62, 64-66, 68, **74, 84, 92, 100, 119, 135, 142, 158, 159,** 182, **202**
Clermont-Ferrand 65
Cleverly, Tony 20, **95**
Collins, Peter 10, 11, 15, 17, 18, 22, **27, 28, 30, 41,** 43, 44, 63
Cologne 9
Commer 14, **70**
Connaught 17
Connaught B type 15
Constructor's World Championship 16, 18, 43, 62, 66, 68
Coombs, John 49, **104, 105, 107**
Cooper 22, 43, 46, 55, 59-61, 66-68
Cooper Climax 81, 86, **92, 93**
Cooper Climax T66 **116**
Cooper, Charles 43
Cooper Formula III **78**
Cooper, John 43
Cooper Maserati 50, **74**
Cooper Monaco **150**
Cooper Special **93**
Cooper T86B 68
Cooper type 53 **72**
Cooper-BRM V12 86B **177**
Cooper-Formula 2 20
Costin, Frank 16
Courage, Piers 68
Coventry 12, 23
Coventry Climax 43, 59, 61, **81**
Crombac, Gerard 'Jabby' **93**
Crystal Palace 51, 52
Cuoghi, Ermano **191**
Curran, Sir Charles 64

Daigh, Chuck 42
Daily Express International Trophy 66
Daily Express Trophy Meeting 9
Daily Mail 66
Daily Telegraph 10
Daily Telegraph Aintree 200 67
Dance, Bob **158**
Dei "Mimmo" **115**
Depailler, Patrick **184**
Dijon **196**
Dodge Drophead Coupé 12
Donald, Bill 13
Dragoni, Eugenio **120, 130**
Driver's World Championship 43, 62, 68
Dubois 36
Duce, Dante 59
Duke, Geoff **74**
Dunlop 45, **80, 111, 126**
Durex 64
Dutch Grand Prix 9, 16, 43, 51, 54, 66, **135**

Eagle 48, 61, **152, 167**
Earl of March 51
Eason-Gibson, John **29, 41**
Ecclestone, Bernie **194**
Ecurie Ecosse 20, **34, 147**
Eifel 9
Elford, Vic 68, **176**
Embassy Racing with Graham Hill **193**
Endruweit, Jim **84**
Ensign Cosworth **189**
Equipe Endeavour 49, **71, 104, 109, 110**
Equipe Nationale Belge **36, 40,** 63, **161**
Evans, Kenneth **29**
Evening News 22

Facel Vega 57, **88, 118**
Fairman, Jack 23, **34, 36**
Fangio, Juan 9, 10, **10,** 11, 15, **24,** 45, 47, 182
Farina, Dr Guiseppe 15, 16
Farnham, Surrey 22
Ferguson 42
Ferrari 10, 11, 15, 16, 18-20, 22, **26, 40,** 42, 43, 45, 47-49, 51-55, 57, 59, 61, 63, 64, 67, **78, 83, 113, 114, 154, 160, 165, 174, 175,** 182, **189, 190, 195, 200**
Ferrari 1512 **201**

Ferrari 156 42, 56, **81, 83, 113, 116, 119, 120, 137**
Ferrari 158 **201**
Ferrari 2.4 **51**
Ferrari 250 GT **105**
Ferrari 250 GTO 49
Ferrari 250 LM **157**
Ferrari 250P 53, **59, 124, 131, 134 140, 142**
Ferrari 275 LM **156**
Ferrari 312 **173**
Ferrari 312 B3 **184, 186**
Ferrari 312 T4 **195**
Ferrari 330 LM **128, 129**
Ferrari 330 P 58
Ferrari 330 P4 51, 63, **64, 160, 161**
Ferrari 375 9, 62
Ferrari 512S 49
Ferrari 625 9
Ferrari D246 **28, 41, 72, 73, 76**
Ferrari Dino 246 42
Ferrari GTO **84, 105-108**
Ferrari GTO 'Drogo' **147**
Ferrari Scuderia **124, 135**
Ferrari Testa Rossa **32, 38-40,** 58, **102, 103, 137**
Ferrari type 500 56
Ferrari V6 **30**
Ferrari, Dino 63
Ferrari, Enzo 16, 42, 49, 51, 63, 64, **81, 194**
FFSA 65
Fiat 51
Fiorano 63
Fittipaldi, Emerson **182, 192**
Flockhard, Ron 18
Flugplatz 9, **24**
Folkingham 9
Ford 51, 61
Ford Cortina **123**
Ford Galaxie 61, **146, 147**
Ford GT40 51, 53, 67, **156**
Ford II, Henry 51
Ford MkII 51
Ford MkIV 51
Ford of America 50, 51, 53
Ford Prefect 12, **18**
Ford Zephyr 10, **27**
Ford-Cosworth 61, 62, 65
Ford-Cosworth V8 48, 66, 182
Ford-Cosworth V8 DFV **167**

Forghieri, Mauro **81, 83, 118, 130, 186, 188**
Formula Libre 15-17
Foyt, A. J. 51
Francis, Alf **20,** 95
French Grand Prix 44, 49, 51, 58, 65, **67, 69, 137, 139, 141, 144, 166, 196**
French Grand Prix French Matra 66
Fry, Ron **157**

Garlits, Don 59
Gemini 46
Gemini Formula Junior **74**
Gendebien, Olivier 20, **38**
German Grand Prix 9, **10,** 11, 14, **24,** 44, **90, 92**
Germany 15
Gethin, Peter **183**
Ginther, Jean **87**
Ginther, Richie 52, **80, 91, 99, 113, 122**
Godia, Francesco **33**
Godin de Beaufort, Carel **90, 114**
Gold Leaf Team Lotus 64
Gonzalez, Froilan 9, 62
Goodwood 17, 18, 22, **20, 30,** 43, 44, 49, 51, 56, 61, 67, **81, 133, 137**
Gould, Horace **27**
Gozzi, Franco **81**
Grand Prix de l'Automobile Club de France 17, 56, 65
Grand Prix Drivers Association 19
Grand Prix Medical Service 19
Gregory, Masten **34,** 59, **81, 84, 87, 88**
Gruber's Restaurant **32**
Guards Trophy **51,** 61, **100, 154**
Guichet, Jean **129**
Gunther, Richie 42
Gurney, Dan **32,** 45, 47-49, 51, 55, 60, **77, 98, 100, 135, 152, 167**

Halford, Bruce **37, 109, 110**
Hall, Jim 55
Hanstein, H. von **100**
Hawthorn, Mike 9, 11, 15-16, 22, **28-30,** 41, 44-46, 55,
Heath, John 20
Herrmann, Hans **26, 33**
Hill, Arthur **70, 80, 84, 99, 115**
Hill, Graham 18, 19, 42, 43, 45-47, 49, 52, 53, 57-62, 65, 68, **70, 79, 80, 84, 91, 99, 104, 105, 113,** 114, 122, 151, 202
Hill, Phil 20, **38, 41,** 42, 47, 53-57, 59, **72, 73, 127, 132, 134, 135, 136, 137, 139, 141**
Hillman Imp 49
Hoare, Col Ronnie 62, **107, 202**
Hobbs, David 53, 68, **123**
Hockenheim 22, 65, 68
Honda 61, 67, 68
Honda France 68
Honda RA 301 **169, 171**
Honda RA 302 **170**
Honda V8 67, 68
Honda V12 67
Honda, Soichiro 67
Honfleur 46, **49**
Howe, Earl **41**
Hugenholtz, John 55
Hulme, Denny 52, 61, 62, 65, 66, 68, **111, 156, 168, 179, 183**
Humber Super Snipe 14
Hunaudières, Les **121**
HWM 20

Ickx, Jackie 67, **69,** 173, 176, 184, 185
Indianapolis 51, 65
Indianapolis 500 56, 60, 61, 68, 182
Indianapolis Ford V8 61
Indycar 48
Intercontinental 42
Intercontinental Formula **77**
International Trophy **28, 29, 41, 70, 77, 79,** 113
International Trophy Race 66
Ireland, Innes 20, 49, 60, **83, 87, 128, 133**
Issigonis, Alec 14
Italian Grand Prix 55, 66, 68
Italian Serenissima V8 61
Ivo, Tommy 59

Jabouille, J. P. **196**
Jaguar 22, 52, 53, **104, 111**
Jaguar 3.4 **28, 29**
Jaguar 3.8 49, **51,** 61, **71, 109, 110**
Jaguar D Type 20, 21, **34, 36,** 76
Jaguar E Type 15, 58, **104, 105, 137**
Jaguar SS 14
James 23
JAP, 500cc 43
Jenkinson Denis 'Jenks' 15, 18, 19, 44, 53, **100**

John Player Special 72 **182, 185**
John Willment Automobiles **146**
Jowett Javelin 13

Karusell 9, 10
Kerr, Phil **168**
Kerrison, Chris **147**
Kessler, Peter **32**
Kimberly, Bill **150**
Klementaski, Louis **99**
Kling, Karl 45

l'Automobile Club de Champagne 45, 59
Lancia Ferrari D50 9, **24, 26,** 60, 99
Lauda, Niki 182, **186, 189, 191, 194**
Lawrence, Jock **34**
Le Man 250P 49
Le Mans 19, 20, 22, 23, **31, 40,** 42, 45, 47, 51, 52, 54, 55, 57, 63, 67, 68, **121, 134, 142**
Lea Francis 14hp 12
Levegh, Pierre 19
Lewis-Evans, Stuart 16, 44
Leyland Tiger 46, **70, 94**
Lister Jaguar **36, 37**
Lloyd, Nevil 56
Lola 46, 53, 67
Lola Climax **78, 89**
Lola Climax 47, 48
Lola-Climax V8 MkIV 45
Lola Cosworth V8 370 **192**
Lola GT 52-54, **123, 149**
Lola T70 53, 61, **155, 158**
Lombank Trophy **78**
London 12, 14, 18, 20-23, 182
Lotus 182
Lotus 42, 46, 47, 53, 57, 61, 64-66, 68, 182
Lotus 18 20, 42, **77**
Lotus 18/21 43, **81**
Lotus 19 44, **81**
Lotus 23B 51, 60
Lotus 24 46, 57, **81, 84, 87, 91, 92, 95,** 141
Lotus 25 43, 45, 47, 49, 55, **86, 118, 119, 135**
Lotus 30 61
Lotus 33 60
Lotus 49 62
Lotus 49B 57, 66, **178**
Lotus 72C 66
Lotus Climax 24, 33 47, **202**

Lotus Cortina 52, 60, **157, 158**
Lotus Elite 21
Macklin, Lance 20
Maggs, Tony 59, **78, 86, 117**
Maglioli, Umberto **124**
Mairesse, Willy **40,** 53, 55, 63, **113, 116, 118, 124, 161**
Maranello 50, 62, **169, 165, 186**
Maranello Concessionaires 49, 52, 54, 62, **107, 128, 202**
Marchetti, Adelmo **39, 73, 76**
Marsh, Anthony 67, **86**
Maserati 11, 17, 18, 43, 58, 61, **139**
Maserati 150S **26**
Maserati 151 57, **101, 134, 139**
Maserati 250F 9, 10, 15, 17, **27,** 42 47, 56, 65
Maserati 3 litre **33**
Maserati 4-CLT 11
Maserati 61 **139**
Maserati France **101**
Maserati V12 43, 67, 68, **153**
Matchless 23
Matra 67
Matra International 48, 66, 68
Matra V12 68
Matra V12 MS11 **180**
Matra-Sports 68
Mays, Raymond 17, **90, 91**
McLaren M2B **153**
McLaren M3A/2 **20**
McLaren M7A **167**
McLaren, Bruce 43, 46, 55, 61, 65, 66, **81, 86, 92, 117, 128, 133, 153, 167, 168, 169**
McLaren-Cosworth V8 M23 **183, 192**
McLaren-Elva **154**
Mecom, John **149**
Mecom, John 53
Mercedes Benz 9, 10, 11, 17, 48
Mercedes-Benz 300SLR 19
Mercedes-Benz W196 45
Merzario, Arturo **184**
Mexican Grand Prix 67
MG Magnette 14
Mini Cooper 43, 60, 111
Miscellaneous memorabilia **197-199**
Modena 9, 10, 17, 62, 63, **146**
Molyslip Trophy **51, 105**
Monaco 18, 19, 42, 44, 51, 56, 60, 62, 63, 65

Monaco Grand Prix 56
Montezemola, Luca di **186, 188**
Monza 9, 15, 42, 50, 55, 61, 66-68, **185**
Moroccan Grand Prix 44
Morris 12
Morris Minor 14
Moss, Alfred 43
Moss, Bill 46
Moss, Stirling 9, 10, 14-16, 17, 20, 22, 23, **26, 33, 35,** 42-44, 60, **71, 75, 81, 85, 133**
Motor Racing Developments **194**
Motor Sport 15, 18, 23, 47
Motor, The 42, 53
Musso, Luigi 44-46, 63

Nancy, Tony 59
Naples Grand Prix 42
Naylor, Brian **37**
New Zealand Grand Prix 64
Noblet, Pierre **129**
Normand Racing Team **139**
North American Racing Team (NART) **32**
Northamptonshire 11
Norton, 500cc 43
Nürburgring 9-11, 22, 23, **24,** 42, 44, 45, 60, **90, 97**

Oliver, Jackie 66, **178**
Oulton Park Gold Cup 42, 45
Owen Racing Organisation 17, 18
Owen, Sir Alfred 16-18, 43, 52

Pabst, Augie 53, **149**
Pace, Carlos **194**
Page & Moy 19
Parkes, Mike 49, 50, **50,** 57, **59, 84, 108, 110, 112, 124, 126, 130, 140, 142, 174**
Parnell, Reg **33, 78**
Parnell, Tim **172**
Pau 44
Peco Trophy **51, 105**
Penske, Roger **150**
Perkins, Denis **152, 172**
Perouse, Monsieur 46, 56
Peterson, Ronnie **185**
Pierpoint, Roy **109**
Piper, David **156**
Pippbrook Garage 20
Podington Airfield 59

Porsche 15, 18, 45, 47, 48, 53, 61, 65, 67
Porsche 1600 RSK **33**
Porsche 1600S 21
Porsche 4 cylinder **78, 81, 90**
Porsche 917 49
Porsche flat 8 **97, 98**
Porsche RS **26**
Porsche type 804 47
Potago, Alfonso de **26**
Prescott 60
Protheroe, Dick 58, **104, 137**

Race of Champions 66, **182, 183, 185**
Racing Car Show 52
Raventlow, Lance 42
Rea, Chris **137**
Reedman, Len 46, **114**
Regazzoni, Gianclaudio 'Clay' 19, **189, 190, 194**
Reims 22, 44-47, 49, 51, 56, 57, **137, 139, 141, 144**
Reims Grand Prix **47, 85, 94**
Remagen 9
Renault RS10 **196**
Reutemann, Carlos **194**
Riley 1.5 litre 12
Rindt, Jochen 65, 66, 68, **153, 179**
Riverside, California 42
Roche, Raymond 'Toto' 58, **60**
Rodriguez, Pedro **172**
Rootes Group 14, 49
Rossfeld 65
Rotary Watches 18
Rouen 44, 46-48, 67, 68
Rouen-les-Essarts 44, 46, 47, 49, 64-66, **67, 97, 99, 166, 181**
Rouselle **36**
Rover 52
Rover 12 12
Rover 90 14
Rover-BRM 52-54, **122**
Rubery Owen & Co Ltd 16
Rubery Owen Holding Ltd 18
Rudd, Tony 57, 6, **91, 99**1
Ryan, Peter 46

Salmon, Mike **76, 128, 156**
Salvadori, Roy 23, 45, 52, **71, 75, 78, 89, 105, 150, 153**
San Sebastian 15

Sanderson, Ninian **34**
Santa Pod 59
Sauber 19
Scalextric Trophy **84**
Scammel, Dick **84**
Scarab 42
Scarfiotti, Ludovico 50, 53, 55, 59, 65, **124, 130, 134, 140**
Scheckter, Jody **184, 195**
Schell, Harry 17, 18
Schlesser, Jo 57, 67, 68, **139, 170**
Schofield, Stanley 56
Scott-Brown, Archie 44
Scott-Watson, Ian 21
Scuderia Centro-Sud **74, 115**
Scuderia Filipinetti 57, **141**
Scuderia SSS Republica di Venezia **81, 102, 105**
Seagrove, Henry 15
Sears, Jack 60, **71, 110, 128, 146**
Seidel, Wolfgang **78**
Serenissima V8 **153**
Servoz-Gavin, Johny **177**
Shelby, Carol 23
Siffert, Jo 19, 57
Silverstone 9, 10, 16-18, **18, 28, 41**, 44, 57, 59, 60, 62, 66, 67, **70, 77, 79**, 113, **116, 146, 184, 195, 196, 200**
Silverstone International Trophy 15
Silverstone Trophy Meeting 16-18
Simon, André 57, **134, 139**
Singer Popular **23**
Sismey, John **122**
Six Hours, *The Motor* **109**
Smith, John 13
Snetterton 44, **78**
Soissons 56
Soissons Straight 45, 59, **85**
Solitude 45
Solitude Grand Prix 47
Sopwith, Sir Thomas **110**
Sopwith, Tommy 28, 49, 71, 110
South African Grand Prix 42
South America 10
Southcott, Willy **113**

Spa Francorchamps 19, 44, 48, 50, 51, 56
Spanish Grand Prix 22, 65
Spence, Mike 55, 65
Standard Vanguard 13
Stanley BRM 18
Stanley, Jean 18
Stanley, Louis 19
Stewart, Sir Jackie 19, 53, 66, 68, **152, 182, 202**
Stuttgart 45
Sunbeam 15
Sunbeam Alpine 14
Sunbeam Rapier 46, 57
Sunbeam Talbot 14
Sunbeam Talbot 90 **13**
Surtees Lola **78**
Surtees, John 45-47, 49, 52, 53, 55, 59, 61, 64, 67, 68, **78, 89, 107, 108, 113, 114, 119, 120, 124, 140, 153, 155, 169, 170, 171,** 182, **201**
Swanley 21
Switzerland 19
Syracuse 50
Syracuse Grand Prix 15, 42
Syrett, Nick 20, 22

Tavoni, Romulo 54, **73**
Taylor, Sid **156**
Taylor, Trevor 47, 52, **91**
Team Lotus 65, 68
Team Surtees Ltd **155**
Thillois 45
Thillois Hairpin **85, 91**
Thin Wall Bearings 16
Thin Wall Special 16
Thompson, John **184**
Thruxton 51
Tomaso, Alessandro de **146**
Tomaso, de **146**
Tour de France Automobile 44
Tourist Trophy 49, 58, 67
Trintignant, Maurice 47, **75, 95**
Triumph
Triumph Mayflower 13
Triumph Renown 13
Triumph TR3 21

Tyrrell 182
Tyrrell Cosworth V8 007 **78, 184**
Tyrrell, Ken 48, 66, **78**

UDT-Laystall 49, **81, 83, 87**
UDT-Laystall Lotuses 45
Upsett, Major 42

van Damn, Sheila 14
Vandervell Products Ltd 14, 16
Vandervell, G. A. (Tony) 14, 16, 17, 46
Vanwall 14-18, 22, 65
Vanwall Special 15, 16
Villeneuve, Giles 63, 182, **195**
Villiers 23
Volkswagen 1200 62
Volkswagen 1500 62
von Trips, 'Taffy' 42

Walker, Johnny 20
Walker, Rob 20, 22, 42, 47, 57, 64, **81, 88, 93, 95, 118, 136**
Watkins Glen 61
Watson, John **182**
Webb, John **155**
Weber **146**
Werra 14
Weslake, Harry 48
Wharton, Ken 16
White, Derek **153, 155**
Whitehead, Graham 20
Whitehead, Peter 20, **36**, 44
Wildes Schwein 10, **27**
Wilkinson, Wilkie **36**
Willment, John 61
Woolworths 42
Wyer, John **132, 150**

Yardley 18, 64

Zandvoort 9, 18, 43, 44, 51, 54-57, 62, 66, 68, **135**
Zeiss, Carl 14
Zeltweg 55
Zerex Special **150**